H. C. G. (Handley Carr Glyn) Moule

Veni Creator

Thoughts on the Person and Work of the Holy Spirit of Promise

H. C. G. (Handley Carr Glyn) Moule

Veni Creator
Thoughts on the Person and Work of the Holy Spirit of Promise

ISBN/EAN: 9783744664813

Printed in Europe, USA, Canada, Australia, Japan

Cover: Foto ©Lupo / pixelio.de

More available books at **www.hansebooks.com**

VENI CREATOR

VENI CREATOR:

THOUGHTS ON THE PERSON AND WORK OF THE HOLY SPIRIT OF PROMISE.

BY THE REV.

H. C. G. MOULE, M.A.,

PRINCIPAL OF RIDLEY HALL, AND FORMERLY FELLOW OF TRINITY COLLEGE, CAMBRIDGE ;

Author of "Thoughts on Christian Sanctity," "On Union with Christ," "On the Spiritual Life," "Outlines of Christian Doctrine," "Secret Prayer," etc.

FOURTH THOUSAND.

London :

HODDER AND STOUGHTON,

27, PATERNOSTER ROW.

———

MDCCCXC.

Printed by Hazell, Watson, & Viney, Ld., London and Aylesbury.

I INSCRIBE THIS BOOK

TO

THE DEAR AND HOLY MEMORY

OF

MY FATHER AND MY MOTHER.

IN WHOM THE SPIRIT OF GOD DWELT

AND

THROUGH WHOM HE WORKED.

———

H. M.
1801 — 1880.
M. M. M.
1801 — 1877.

———

IN PACE.

———

"Yea, saith the Spirit; that they may rest from their labours, and their works do follow them."

"Thou holy Spirite, we pray to the
Strengthe our fayth and increase it alwaye;
Comforth our hertes in adversite
With trewe beleve bothe nyght and daye.
Kirieleyson.

"Thou worthy lyght, that art so cleare,
Teache us Christe Jesu to knowe alone;
That we have never cause to feare
In hym to have redempcyon.
Kirieleyson.

"Thou swete love, graunt us altogether
To be unfayned in charite ;
That we may all love one another,
And of one mynde alwaye to be.
Kirieleyson.

"Be thou our comfortoure in all nede ;
Make us to feare nether death nor shame;
But in the treuth to be stablyshed,
That Sathan put us not to blame.
Kirieleyson."

Bishop Coverdale, 1488—1569.

PREFACE.

THE subject of the following chapters needs no prefatory introduction to the Christian reader. In itself eternally and divinely important, it has become in the mercy of God a special subject of our own time. Far and wide in the Christian Church, amidst too many phenomena of peril and perplexity, we hail as a phenomenon of good and glorious omen an ever-deepening attention to the divine promises which gather round the truth of the Holy Ghost. More and ever more it is recognized by those who name the Name of the SON that, alike for individual blessing and for the work and witness of the Community, we depend with an absolute need upon the presence and power of the SPIRIT.

May these pages, for all their fragmentary character, be used in some measure by HIM of whom they speak to stir up His saints so always to lay hold on Him that He evermore may lay hold on them, and graciously fill them with Himself.

CAMBRIDGE,
March 28th, 1890.

CONTENTS.

CHAPTER III.

CHAPTER IV.

CHAPTER V

CHAPTER VI.

CHAPTER VII.

CHAPTER X.

CHAPTER XI.

CHAPTER XII.

CHAPTER I.

THE following chapters have a very simple purpose. They are not intended to constitute a technical treatise, certainly not to carry the reader into elaborate enquiries into the history of doctrines. They are intended to be a reverent review of some, and only some, of the main teachings of the Holy Scriptures concerning the ever-blessed Spirit of God, the heavenly Paraclete, the eternal Third Person, the Lord and Life-Giver, and His revealed work in Redemption. And this review shall be made, by His most merciful assistance, with a constant reference to the actual needs of the human soul, the actual experience of the people of God.

The theme is one of altogether special importance for the believing Church of these latter days. In John Owen's *Pneumatologia*, his deep, massive, and most spiritual " Discourse

Concerning the Holy Spirit" (1674), occurs a remarkable passage (bk i., ch. i.), in which he traces through the ages and dispensations a certain progress of divine tests of living orthodoxy, related to each of the Three Persons in succession.   Before the First Advent the great testing truth was "the oneness of God's nature and His monarchy over all," with special respect to the Person of the Father.   At the First Advent the great question was whether a Church orthodox on the first point would now receive the divine Son, incarnate, sacrificed, and glorified, according to the promise.   And when the working of this test had gathered out the Church of Christian believers, and built it on the foundation of the truth of the Person and Work of the Lord Jesus Christ, then the Holy Spirit came in a new prominence and speciality before that Church as a touchstone of true faith.   "Wherefore the duty of the Church now immediately respects the Spirit of God, who acts towards it in the name of the Father and of the Son ; and with respect unto Him it is that the Church in its present state is capable of an apostasy from God. . . . The sin of despising His Person and rejecting His Work now is of the same nature with idolatry of old, and with the Jews' rejection of the Person of the Son."

The statement is perhaps too absolute in form to embrace all the data of revelation and experience. But it is at least an indication of great spiritual facts, and a solemn caution to the Christian of the present day to take heed lest he lose hold of the truth of the blessed Spirit in its humbling but beatifying fulness. All too easily, amidst prevalent fashions of opinion in the modern Church, we may insensibly, unconsciously, let that truth fall from us. We may take up with a view of human nature in its fallen estate which shall practically dispense with the need of the regenerating and sanctifying Holy Ghost. We may take up with a view of sacred order and divine ordinances which shall in effect put His sovereign and mysterious work into other hands than His. May He, the Lord, the Life-Giver, personal, sovereign, loving, mighty, preserve us from unfaithfulness of regard towards His blessed Person, from untruth of view of His divine work. May He keep us

indeed "men of the Spirit," filling us, that we
may be so, with Himself.

As we approach our subject more immediately, let us very deliberately take the attitude
of invocation and adoration. Who can rightly
think and discourse about the Holy Spirit of
God save by that same Spirit, and as seeking
with humblest reverence to follow the very
syllables and footsteps. of that written Word
which has Him everywhere for its true
Author?

It is recorded in the story of the German
Reformation that on one of its most memorable
occasions, the disputation between Eck and
Luther before Duke George of Saxony at the
castle of the Pleissenburg, the controversy was
preluded by the solemn chant of the *Veni
Creator*, sung thrice over while the whole as-
sembly knelt.[1] With the voices of the soul
may we, writer and reader, so now unite, as we
approach not a great battle of arguments but a

---

[1] D'Aubigné, *Hist. de la Réformation du* XVIme *Siècle, liv.* v.,
ch. iv. Köstlin, *Luthers Leben*, p. 149.

series of quiet meditations upon the Person and
the Work of the Lord the Spirit.

> " Veni, Creator Spiritus,
>   Mentes tuorum visita ;
>   Imple superna gratia
>   Quæ Tu creasti pectora ;
>
> " Qui Paraclitus diceris,
>   Altissimi donum Dei,
>   Fons vivus, Ignis, Caritas,
>   Et spiritalis Unctio." [1]

In the present chapter I propose to speak of
the revealed PERSONALITY of the Holy Spirit
as the all-important preliminary to all other
thoughts concerning Him.   Upon His Divinity,
His Deity, there is little practical need that I

---

[1] Rendered thus among the " Hymns " formerly appended to
the Prayer Book :—

> " Come, Holy Ghost, Creator, come,
>   And visit all the souls of Thine ;
>   Thou hast inspired our hearts with life,
>   Inspire them now with life divine.
>
> " Thou art the Comforter, the Gift
>   Of God most High, the Fire of love,
>   The everlasting Spring of joy,
>   And holy Unction from above."

See the whole ancient hymn in Trench's *Sacred Latin Poetry*,
p. 184.   It appears to be certainly older than its reputed author,
Charlemagne.   See too the beautiful hymn to the Holy Spirit by
King Robert the Second of France (A.D. 997), *ibid*, p ·196.

should dwell, so plain it is on the very surface of Scripture that the Holy Spirit, whether personal or not, is divine, is a Power of the divine Order. But is it HE, or IT? Is it a divine faculty, influence, phase, mode, or a divine Person?

Now the most direct answer to this question, and at the same time the deepest and tenderest, is to go at once to the central passage of all Scripture in the matter. All over the blessed Book from its very first lines onward lie scattered mentions of the Spirit and His work. Here and there we have passages which go almost the length of revealing explicitly His personality; here and there passages which fully go that length, fairly interpreted. But there is one precious section of Scripture which is to these scattered rays as their combining focus, the glorious ruling passage of the subject. And where and what is it? Not some great chapter of apostolic argument and exposition, such as those in which the Godhead of the Son is asserted, or the holy paradox of Justification by Faith explained and applied to the trembling, weary conscience and longing heart. No; for the decisive teaching on the Personality of the

Holy Ghost we go yet deeper into the Scripture tabernacle ; we enter its Holiest ; we open the pages where the Lord Jesus Himself teaches with His own lips the secrets of spiritual life. There, as it were under the John xiv.-xvi. Shechinah itself, lies our doctrinal stronghold for this article of faith. There speaks the Christ of God, in an hour of supreme tenderness, and from which all ideas of the rhetorical and the merely poetical are infinitely distant ; and He speaks with repetition and emphasis of this same Holy Spirit, and He speaks of Him as personal. My readers are well aware of the fact. But it is never in vain to impress such a fact again upon the soul by re-examination of the infallible words. Let me ask that the Greek be once more opened, and this divine grammatical anomaly once more studied—the neuter Πνεῦμα associated repeatedly and markedly with the masculine Παράκλητος, the John xiv. 16, 17; masculines ὅς, ἐκεῖνος, αὐτός.[1] And xv. 26 ; xvi. 7, 8. let this be read in the light of the wonderful context, in which this blessed *Paraclete*, this

---

[1] And if the question is asked, what language did the Lord Jesus speak that night, Greek or Aramaic ; and if Aramaic, how

Advocatus,[1] " called in " to the aid of the otherwise " orphaned " Church, is seen to be such,
and to act so, as to be indeed the Substitute, the
more than substitute, for the unspeakably real
personality of the Saviour in His seen presence.
The passage sets the Holy Spirit before us as
not the Father, as not the Son, and yet as the
" Vicar of Christ " (the phrase is Tertullian's[2]),
the ample Consolation for the absence of the
familiar company of the beloved Saviour.   It
scarcely needs the impressive testimony of the
Greek grammar of the sentences to assure us
with deep and restful certainty that to the mind
of the Saviour that night the Spirit was indeed
present as a Person.

In this central and decisive passage then we
have the Holy Ghost revealed to us in so many

was the contrast between masculine and neuter conveyed? we
reply that the question, most interesting and important in itself,
is not in point in our enquiry.   For us as believers in the divine
character of the Written Word the discourses of the New Testament, and of the Old Testament too, are before us as *reports
corrected and edited by the Author.*

[1] For a vindication of the rendering *Advocate* for *Paracletus*
see Lightfoot, *On a Fresh Revision of the N.T.*, pp. 50-56
Meantime the dear familiar word Comforter, *Confortator*, remains
as a true *paraphrase* of Paraclete.

[2] *De Virginibus Velandis*, c. I.

words as Him, not only as It; as the living and conscious Exerciser of true personal will and love, as truly and fully as the First 1 John ii. 1. "Paraclete," the Lord Jesus Christ Himself. And now this central passage radiates out its glory upon the whole system and circle of Scripture truth about the Spirit. From Gen. i. 2 to Rev. xxii. 17 it sheds the warmth of divine personal life into every mention of the blessed Power.[1] With the Paschal Discourse in our heart and mind, we know that it was He, not It, who "brooded" over the primeval deep. He, not It, "strove with man," or Gen. i. 2. "ruled in man," of old. He, not Gen. vi. 3. It, was in Joseph in Egypt, and Gen. xli. 38. upon Moses in the wilderness of Numb. xi. 17. wandering, and upon judges and kings of

---

[1] I well know that it is maintained that in the Greek New Testament, as a rule, τὸ Πνεῦμα denotes the Personal Paraclete, and πνεῦμα without the article not the Person but the influence. With some exceptions I believe this rule holds good. But it leaves quite untouched the line of reasoning in the text here. When we have ascertained that τὸ Πνεῦμα is indeed a Person we know that πνεῦμα is a *personal influence*. And in the general light of Scripture teaching on divine Influences we are abundantly secure in saying that this means nothing less than *the divine Person at work.*

after-days. He, not It, "spake by the prophets," "moving" those "holy men of God." He, not It, drew the plan of the ancient Tabernacle and of the first Temple. He, not It, lifted Ezekiel to his feet in the hour of vision. He, not It, came upon the Virgin, and anointed her Son at Jordan and led Him to the desert of temptation, and gave utterance to the saints at Pentecost, and caught Philip away from the road to Gaza, and guided Paul through Asia Minor to the nearest port for Europe. He, not It, effects the new birth of regenerate man, and is the Breath of his new life, and the Earnest of his coming glory. By Him, not by It, the believer walks, and mortifies the deeds of the body, filled not with It, but Him. He, not It, is the Spirit of faith, by whom it is "given unto us to believe on Christ." He, not It, speaks to the Churches. He, not It, says from heaven that they who die in the

Judges vi. 34.
1 Sam. x. 10.
1 Sam. xxii. 2.
2 Kings ii. 9, 15.
2 Chron. xv. 1.
Matt. xxii. 43.
Heb. x. 15.
1 Peter i. 11.
2 Peter i. 21.
Heb. ix. 8.
1 Chron. xxviii. 12.
Ezek. ii. 2.
Luke i. 35.
Luke ii. 22.
Luke iv. 1.
Acts ii. 4.
Acts viii. 39.
Acts xvi. 6, 7.
John iii. 5, 6, 8.
Gal. v. 25.
Rom. viii. 11.
Eph. i. 13, 14.
Gal. v. 25.
Rom. viii. 13.
Eph. v. 18.
2 Cor. iv. 13.
Phil. i. 29.
Rev. ii. 7, 11, 29; iii. 6, 13, 22.

Lord are blessed, and calls in this Rev. xiv. 13.
life upon the wandering soul of man to come
to the living water. Rev. xxii. 17.

And let us not wonder, by the way, that the
exhibition of His Personality is comparatively
so reserved in Scripture ; that we have need,
as in the case of the Personality of the Father
and of the Son we have not at all, to place
Scripture by Scripture and make an induction
on the subject. The reason lies in the nature
of the case. The Holy Spirit is the true
Author of the Written Word ; and Heb. x. 15.
His authorship there is occupied with the
main and absorbing theme not of Himself
but of another Person, the Son of God. Incidentally, like some of His human agents in
the production of the Scriptures—like Moses,
and Jeremiah, and Paul, and John—He dis-
closes enough of His blessed Self to give
us full apprehension of His personal reality ;
but His theme, His burthen, is JESUS CHRIST.
And again in the unfolding and application
of Redemption His work is above all things
secret, internal, subjective. It is to take of
the things of Christ, to deal with the blessed

objectivity of the finished work and inexhaustible riches of Christ, and with inmost touches
and new-creating whispers to manifest them to
the spirit of man.   It is to bring man, by a
divine but inscrutable operation, to believe in
Christ and to possess Him, with a spontaneity
truly man's own while yet Another is in it.   As
to His saving operations, the Spirit lies hidden
as it were behind Christ Jesus and in our own
inner man.   So it is also in measure in His
revelations of Himself in His holy Word.

However this is by the way.   The point
before us now, in the matter of the Personality
of the Spirit, is just this : that we have the
central and open revelation of that personality
given us in Scripture in a place and under circumstances charged with indescribable tenderness and sacredness.   The truth thus appears
not only as a demand on the obedience of faith
—though this it is indeed—but as a gift to the
believing soul of heavenly love, of love deep
and warm as the heart of the Redeemer.

There seems to be a drift and set at the
present day, in many quarters where what are
called liberalizing tendencies in theology prevail,

to discredit, or minimize, or ignore, the belief of
the Personality of the blessed Spirit. In what
interest and to what end, one asks, is such
a tendency accepted or promoted? Surely not
with the hope of presenting the Christian plan,
the process of eternal love and goodness, in
fairer, tenderer, or more living colours and
glories. If a reference to personal experience
may be permitted I may indeed here "set to
my seal." Never shall I forget the gain to
conscious faith and peace which came to my
own soul, not long after a first decisive and ap-
propriating view of the Crucified Lord as the
sinner's Sacrifice of peace, from a more intelli-
gent and conscious hold upon the living and
most gracious Personality of that Holy Spirit
through whose mercy the soul had got that
blessed view. It was a new development of
insight into the Love of God. It was a new
contact as it were with the inner and eternal
movements of redeeming goodness and power,
a new discovery in divine resources. At such
a "time of finding," gratitude, and love, and
adoration gain a new, a newly realized, reason,
and motive-power and rest. He who with

His secret skill, and with a power not the less almighty because it violates nothing, has awakened and regenerated the man, now shines before his inner sight with the smile of a personal and eternal kindness and amity, and is seen standing side by side, in union unspeakable yet without confusion, with Him who has suffered and redeemed, and with Him who laid the mighty plan of grace, and willed its all-merciful success, and spared not His own Son, giving Him over for us all. ·If I may reverently use the simile, it is as when to two notes of the musical triad the related third note is added, and there results, in the words of the music-loving poet, "not a fourth sound, but a star."[1]

As our enquiry proceeds we shall have continual occasion of course to recur to this primary theme, the Personality of the Holy Ghost; and much that is omitted in this preliminary statement will thus be supplied. But we have at least aimed here at the great mark of setting the sacred fact, as a fact, well before us, and letting it take its large place anew in

---

[1] Browning, *Abt Vogler.*

the consciousness, and so in the action, of the believing man.   That place is surely meant to be a large one, in the light of the Paschal Discourse, as we have traced its import.   There the blessed Person of the Paraclete is revealed as just about to fill the void of the disciples' hearts with a whole wealth of personal, gracious action, abiding, revealing, teaching, leading, conveying into the inmost receptacle the presence of Christ, so that He while absent should be present, while invisible should be seen.   Surely such a presence and such an action was intended to call forth on the happy Christian's part a reverent and loving reciprocation.   If thus the Spirit was to deal with him, he was to deal with the Spirit in holy recognition, and adoring gratitude, and confiding love.   " The Spirit with our Rom. viii. 16. spirit " is a phrase meant to carry endless blessed applications in the experiences of the life of faith.

As we close, the question perhaps arises from the thoughts just suggested, whether acts of direct adoration to the Holy Spirit are prescribed to us in the Scriptures.   It is certainly remarkable that we have very little in their pages which bears explicitly on the question, a fact which however falls very naturally in with what we have already seen of the general comparative reticence of the Author of the Book about His own nature and glory. And, again, it is a fact in harmony with what we have seen of the character of His work for the Christian, a work pre-eminently subjective, so profoundly so as to occasion such a·statement as that of St Paul that the Spirit intercedes for the saints Rom. viii. 27. with groanings that cannot be uttered, words whose context at least suggests that the intercession has its action in the region of the inner man, and breathes itself or groans itself forth through the regenerate human spirit. If it is the Holy Spirit's special function not only to speak to and deal with, but also to speak and work through, the man He renews and sanctifies, we can just so far understand that He the less presents Himself for our articulate adoration. But meanwhile the sacred rightfulness of our worship of the Holy Spirit is as surely established as anything can be that rests on large and immediate inferences from the Scriptures. If He is divine, and if He is personal, how can we help the attitude of adoration when, leaving for the moment the thought of His work in us, we isolate in our view the thought of Him the Worker? Scripture practically prescribes to us such an attitude when it gives us our Lord's own account, in His baptismal formula, of the Eternal NAME as His disciples were to know it—" The Name of the Father, and of the Son, and of the Holy Ghost ;" and when in the Acts and the Epistles the Holy Ghost is set before us as not only doing His work in the inmost being of the individual but presiding in sacred majesty over the community ; and when in Acts v. 3. the Revelation He, in the mysti- Acts xiii. 2. Acts xv. 28. cal sevenfoldness of His operation, 1 Cor. xii. 11-13. Seven yet One, appears in that solemn prelude as the concurrent Giver, with the Father and the Son, of grace and peace ; Rev. i. 4. above all when in the Paschal Dis- John xiv. 16. course the adorable and adored Lord Jesus presents Him to our faith as co-ordinate with Himself in glory and grace, "another Comforter."

2

So, while watchfully and reverently seeking
to remember the laws of Scripture proportion,
and that according to it the believer's relation
to the Spirit is *not so much* that of direct adoration as of a reliance which wholly implies it, let
us trustfully and thankfully worship Him, and
ask blessing of Him, as our spirits shall be
moved to such action under His grace.   Let us
ever and again recollect, with deliberate contemplation and faith, .what by His word we
know of Him, and of His presence in us and
His work for us, and then let us not only "pray
Jude 20.   *in* the Holy Ghost" but also *to* Him,
whether in the words of some ancient *Veni*, or
in the many songs of supplication which have
been given us, surely not without His leading,
in these latter days of His gracious dispensation.
One such out of many let me quote and let me
use, breathed from the soul and mind of my
own beloved and Spirit-taught father long ago,
and sung by him (how often! in tones how
well remembered!) in his hours of adoration to
the last :

" Come, Holy Comforter, celestial Light,
   Relieve from all obscurity our sight ;

Come, Holy Comforter, celestial Fire,
Our souls with love and purity inspire ;
Hear, Holy Ghost, our supplicating cry,
Nor leave the grace Thou gav'st to droop and die.

"Come, Holy Comforter, a Saviour's love
Reveal, and fix our hearts on joys above ;
Come, Holy Comforter, the flesh subdue,
And aid us, one with Christ, His will to do ;
Hear, Holy Ghost, our supplicating cry,
Nor leave the grace Thou gav'st to droop and die."

ADDENDUM TO CHAPTER I.

THE SIN OF RAILING ($\beta\lambda\alpha\sigma\phi\eta\mu\iota\alpha$) AGAINST THE HOLY GHOST.

(Matt. xii. 31, 32; Mark iii. 28-30; Luke xii. 10. See Heb. vi. 4-8, x. 26-31 ; 1 John v. 16.)

ON this awful and mysterious subject I offer only a very few words, and these are offered mainly because of the connexion of the subject with that of the Personality of the Holy Spirit. For it appears to be justly reckoned among the proofs of the Personality that this unspeakably dread warning should be given, in which railing against the Spirit is seen as a sin comparable in kind with railing against the holy personal Saviour.

For myself I feel, as surely many a Christian does, how very much easier it is to say what this great acme and last development[1] of sin *is not* than what it is. Whatever it is, it is always and for ever true that the man who as a fact comes penitent to the feet of Christ for pardon finds it. And whatever it is, the Saviour's own words of warning surely imply that it is not, so to speak, a terrible accident of the sinful soul's action but (see Müller cited in the note) a development, the result of a process, the outcome of a deliberately formed condition. In order to it there needs, assuredly, the concurrence of great and God-given *light* upon good and evil, sin and salvation (see Heb. vi.), with a resolved, deliberate, and matured hostility and repulsion on the part of the will ; a personal hatred of recognized eternal holiness.

---

[1] See some excellent remarks on the Unpardonable Sin as being not an isolated sin but sin in its full development, in Julius Müller, *Christian Doctrine of Sin*, T. & T. Clark's Eng. Trans., i., p. 418, etc.

Why is this sin unpardonable? Because, surely, it is such a closing of the door of repentance by the created personality against itself as, by laws of spiritual nature which we cannot analyse but may in part divine, shuts up the personality finally against grace; denies all possible ground, all *nidus*, to the action of Him whom it has in some sense seen and yet deliberately hated. And some further light, if I mistake not, is thrown on this *irremissibility* by the fact that the Gospel, the Dispensation of the Spirit (see *e.g.* 2 Cor. iii. 6-8), is seen in Scripture as the *final* message of divine mercy. He who in the full light of this final Gospel deliberately rejects its message and its Messenger, casts off the *last* offers, the justly and necessarily last, of salvation. No *more* powerful, tender, prevailing secrets of conquest and persuasion lie beyond. This comes out in Heb. x., where the possible apostate back from Christ to antichristian Judaism is warned that no new sacrifice for sin will meet his awful need. The old offerings have done their work for ever; and Calvary will not be repeated. From one point of view we may thus say that

the warnings of the Saviour in the Gospels
mean, in effect, that while a merciful forbear-
ance could, in the nature of things, be extended
for His sake to that rejection of Him which
was committed " in the days of His flesh,"
while He stood before His enemies as pre-
eminently " The Son of MAN," it would be
otherwise when He was deliberately and finally
refused under the dispensation of that Holy
Spirit who should bear ·witness to Him in His
accomplished work and glory as "the Captain
of salvation made perfect."[1]

Can the truly regenerate commit this sin ?
I venture to say *yes*, and *no*.   In themselves,
and as relying more on their regeneration than
their Regenerator, *yes*.   In Him, and under
His covenant of grace, I humbly believe, *no
and never*.   Heb. vi. 4-8, as it appears to me
(the weighty remarks of J. Müller notwithstanding), deals with the case not of the soul
vivified with the divine life of holiness and love
by the Spirit of Christ, but of the soul gifted by
that Spirit with the fullest *light separable from*

---

[1] See Whitby, *On the New Testament, Appendix to St
Matthew xii.*

love. Balaam's recorded condition remarkably illustrates every detail of Heb. vi. 4-8.

Meanwhile let us take heed, watching and praying, not to grieve the Spirit of love and holiness. It is better to be dismayed than to presume. But it is best of all most reverently to trust.

CHAPTER II

VENI CREATOR SPIRITUS, was the thought with which our previous chapter closed. Let us begin again with the same. In following the scriptural traces of the doctrine of the blessed Spirit we will remember that He is the promised "Guide into all the John xvi. 13. truth." By Him we will seek "a right judgment in all things" concerning His revealed glory, such a judgment that we may "evermore rejoice in His holy comfort," the comfort of a happy insight into what He is as Comforter.

I propose to treat in this chapter of two important sides of the doctrine of the Spirit : the Forthcoming of the Spirit in the Holy Trinity from the Father and the Son ("the Dual Procession"), and the work of the Spirit in relation to the Human Nature of our Lord Jesus Christ.

1. The words *Procession of the Spirit* can scarcely be spoken or written without calling up associated thoughts of strife and division within the Christian Church, and the hardly less unhappy remembrance of that ultra-speculative treatment of divine truths which has too often proved a fruitful source of divisions. Not seldom even the most pious and reverent minds have been beguiled into discussing the Nature of God and the eternal Relations of the divine Persons in a tone which would be justified only if we had actually "found out the Almighty unto perfection" and saw   Job xi. 7. before us, arranged in a series of absolutely certain premisses, major and minor, all that HE knows about HIMSELF.   Hence in no small measure arose that great controversy of East and West upon the Dual Procession which led to a final rupture about the year 1050, a rupture never since healed, nay so little healed that as recently as 1863[1] a declaration was issued from Constantinople condemning as heresy the Western belief, confessed

---

[1] See Smeaton, *Doctrine of the Holy Spirit*, p. 289.

in our two longer Creeds and in the Fifth Anglican Article.

But notwithstanding all this it is fully possible, I trust, to treat this subject of the Dual Procession, great and also tender as it is, without either a long discussion of the history of belief[1] or an unconscious imitation of the speculative tendency referred to. All I ask now to do is to take this doctrine, which our Church, both before and after the Reformation, has as a fact avowed to be Scripture truth, and to look upon it in the serene and blessed light of the revealed and experienced work of the Lord the Life-Giver in His ministry for Christ in the Church and in the soul. We shall surely find it to be no mere phantom of abstract and unlicensed speculation, but a truth of life and love.

What then in effect do we mean when we speak of the Procession of the Spirit from the Father and the Son? We mean that in the revealed inner relations of Godhead, in those eternal and necessary relations (" necessary " in the well-understood sense that they are rela-

---

[1] For a brief conspectus of the history I may venture to refer to my *Outlines of Christian Doctrine*, pp. 146, etc.

tions lying in the very Nature of God, relations which in that Nature *must be*, even as holiness *must be* in it), while the Father is the eternal Origin of the Eternal Spirit, the Son is concurrently His eternal Origin also. We mean that Godhead is eternally in the Spirit because of the Son as well as because of the Father. We do not mean that the blessed Son is thus the Spirit's Origin in an independent and separated way. *All* that the Son is, as the Second Person of the Holy Trinity, He is "of the Father," and of the Father alone.[1] To this He bore abundant personal witness "in the days of His flesh." But we John v. 25, etc. believe that the "all" which He thus eternally derives includes *inter alia* this—that He is, with the Father, the concurrent Origin of the Holy Spirit.

Such a humble belief is neither an arbitrary and barren demand upon a bewildered or unreflecting assent, nor a thing so sublimated and vanishing as to find no point of contact with life and love. In the first place, it throws some

---

[1] See Pearson, *Exposition of the Creed*, p. 136, etc.

precious light of its own upon that *Sanctum Sanctorum* of life and love, the inner relations of the Persons of the blessed Godhead. He who is at once the Spirit of the Father and the Spirit of the Son, and One with Both—is He not, in His blessed personal existence, the Result, the Bond, the Vehicle, of Their everlasting mutual delight and love? That such He is was the belief of Christians long ago, a belief resting not indeed upon direct revelation, but upon inferences deep and lawful suggested by it. It is put into articulate statements by St Augustine, in his treatise *On the Trinity*, vi. 5. It falls in with the doctrine of the Dual Procession in a true harmony. And surely the study of anything which casts light on the revelation of that Mutual Love is full of practical blessing to thoughtful faith, for it is a contribution to the study of that inexhausti-

1 John iv. 8, 16. ble text, "GOD IS LOVE." Yes, not only does God do acts of love, however great. In the inmost heart and secret of His Being He "IS LOVE."

And when we come from the revealed inner life of Godhead to the divine work of redemption we find a manifest aid and blessing in the belief of the eternal Forthcoming of the Holy Spirit from the Son as well as from the Father. In the light of this belief, every part and detail of the work of the Spirit in connexion with the Person and work of Christ gains indefinitely in our view in respect of closeness and tenderness of contact. In the light of this belief, He who "testifies of" Christ, and "glorifies" Him, and imparts Him, does all this blessed work not only as the holy Messenger and Co-operator of the Saviour but as the Stream from Him the Fountain. Deep must be the harmonies of such co-operation. Absolute must be the truth and fulness of such testimony. Close, unspeakably close, must be the union effected by such an Intermediary.

Meanwhile the scriptural basis for this belief is strong, and capable of simple statement. In Scripture the Spirit is as freely called "the Spirit of the Son," "the Spirit of Christ," as "the Spirit of God," "the Spirit of the Father." And He is as freely said to be "sent" by the Son as by the Father. But we gather from

Rom. viii. 9.
Gal. iv. 6.
1 Pet. i. 11.
Eph. iii. 16.
Luke xxiv. 49.

Scripture, with abundant fulness, and in many directions, that the works of the blessed Three Persons in redemption bear always a deep and steadfast reference to their eternal inner relations. Thus the Eternal Father of the Son, and not the Son, is the Father of the believer. The Eternal Son, and not the Father, is the First-born among many brethren. Therefore, by the rule of a deep and holy analogy, we believe that the relation of the Spirit to the Son in respect of saving work rests upon their relation in respect of eternal Being. Him who is " the Spirit of the Son, sent by the Son," for us men and for our salvation, we humbly and adoringly believe to be related to the Son in the inner sanctuary of Godhead after the manner of an unbeginning and unending Procession, Forthcoming, of Divine Life.

If such is indeed the truth, let our insight into it rise higher, infinitely higher, than any mere analysis or record, however careful, of a great Church controversy. It is a thing which can and should lead us up to look upon the very springs of life eternal. It is one of the

mighty truths which converge upon the inexhaustible glory and preciousness of our Lord
Jesus Christ ; upon His central position for us
in the plan of salvation ; upon the close connexion with Him, the infinitely close connexion,
of all parts of that plan and work; the parts
which concern our holiness as truly as these
which concern our acceptance.

2. This last thought leads me to a few considerations on our second present topic ; the
work of the Holy Spirit in relation to the
Human Nature of our Lord Jesus Christ.   On
this topic I dwell in order above all to empha-
size some practical spiritual truths about the
Spirit's regenerating and sanctifying work for
us who come to Christ and are in Him.

It is but rapidly, and as collecting specimens
of illustration, that I need remind my readers
of the large and deep connexion revealed in
Scripture between the Holy Spirit and the Son
of Man.

The Holy Spirit was the immediate Agent in
the Immaculate Conception of " that   Luke i. 35.
holy Thing."   Not that He was therefore the

Father of the blessed Son ; but He was the vehicle of the Paternity. Not again that He so acted that the Son as God had nothing to do with the act of the Incarnation. The Son, in divine will, willed to assume our nature, and so assumed it ; but again the blessed Spirit wrought the process whereby that will was carried out. And then, thirty years later, the Spirit descended upon the youthful Lord at His baptism, in some in-

Matt. iii. 16; etc. scrutable speciality of presence and

Luke iv. 1-14. power. In this " power of the Spirit " He went forth first to temptation and then to ministry. It was in the Spirit, "given without measure," that He " spoke the words

John iii. 34. of God." It was "by means of the Eternal Spirit," wonderful phrase, that He

Heb. ix. 14. "offered Himself without spot to God." We find indications that the Spirit had great things to do with the bodily resurrec-

Rom. viii. 11. tion of the buried Lord. After resurrection it was " by the Holy Spirit " that

Acts i. 2. He " gave commandment to the Apostles." And when in the Revelation the glorified Jesus, as the slain One risen again

and ascended, speaks to the seven Churches, the voices of the Saviour and of the Spirit are as one. Rev. ii. 1-7, etc.

With the reserve of humblest reverence, may we not say that the Manhood of our dear Redeemer was produced, and maintained all along in its absolute and unalterable perfection, not by His own action as God the Son but by that of God the Holy Spirit? His own divine act in the matter was, as we have said, and as Owen said long ago,[1] to *assume* the Manhood, but no more. Never indeed, not for one moment from the first, was that Manhood dissociated from the Godhead of the Son. Never for a moment had it a personality independent of that of God the Son. The very Person who said, in the days of His flesh, "Before Abraham was, I am," the Person John viii. 58. who under His great humiliation said to a whole world of sin and sorrow, "Come unto Me," was then and there as truly att. x. 28. GOD[2] as He was before the world was. But

---

[1] See *Pneumatologia*, bk. ii., ch. iii.

[2] And not God in abeyance, as some have seemed to say, giving to His *Kenôsis* (Phil. ii. 7) a meaning not borne out by Scripture. On the theory that He so "made Himself void" as

all this leaves untouched the sacred truth that
the Manhood He took was, in the divine order
and law, manhood begun and maintained in its
perfect holiness and power by the Holy Spirit
as the immediate personal divine Worker. It
is accordingly by the Holy Spirit that the Lord
Jesus Christ is the Second Man. It is by the
Holy Spirit that He, as the Second Man now
glorified, is the Receptacle, the Reservoir, the
Col. i. 19; Fountain-head, of that "all fulness"
ii. 9, 18. which dwells in Him for us.

We pass almost instantly in the treatment
of such a subject into regions beyond our
analysis. But we see enough to deepen and

to become liable to mental error, mistakes of fact and reasoning,
for example about the age and nature of the Old Testament
Scriptures, see by all means Liddon, *Bampton Lectures*, Lecture
viii. It may be enough here to point out that to view such a
voluntary fallibility on our Lord's part as an instance of His
blessed *self-humiliation* involves a certain confusion of concep-
tions. It would stand, supposing it to be true, under a very
different description from, for instance, His voluntary liability to
fatigue, sorrow, and death. A rich and refined philanthropist,
bent on elevating a degraded tribe, would give a beautiful instance of self-humiliation in consenting, if it were expedient, to be
as poor, and as badly lodged, as they. But if, while coming as
their teacher, he consented to share their ignorance (were it
possible) on matters on which he undertook to teach them, he
would deprive himself to their loss and disadvantage.

strengthen our "faith in the operation of God," to impart a growing definite- Col. ii. 12.
ness of view, and a fuller peace in the heart, and a more humble adoration, as we ponder our own transition, by the power of the Spirit, "from death unto life," and onwards John v. 24; always to "life more abundant." x. 10.

For in this recollection of the truth of the Spirit's work on and in the Manhood of our blessed Head we are brought directly to a fuller recollection also of the PLACE OF CHRIST (if I may express myself so) in the Holy Spirit's saving work for us. Let us take this up as our closing topic for this chapter.

We who believe indeed in the Lord Jesus Christ know on the evidence of God's Word that we owe our saving faith to the Lord the Spirit, "the Spirit of faith." We 2 Cor. iv. 13.
who were once "dead in trespasses Eph. ii. 1.
and sins," and who now live, know on the same evidence that we were, in "abundant mercy," "born of the Spirit," and John iii. 8.
that every step which we take in that life we take "by the Spirit." Is the Gal. v. 25.
"sound" of regenerate vitality and action

"heard," in however small a whisper yet *audibly*, in our souls and in the outward life which manifests their condition ? It is the blessed Spirit's presence in special grace. It is the evidence, the one evidence, of our real new birth, new creation, by Him. I say, it is the one evidence of this. For let us remember that across all the problems of sacramental operation we must read always those words of our Lord about the mystic Wind. Wherever that *Wind* is, yes, wherever it is, by its very nature as wind *it moves*; it is not merely latent ; it is heard : " Thou hearest the sound thereof ; *so is every one* that is born of the Spirit." But on this I do not linger now.[1] Our concern now is with the experiences of the life of grace in Christ, and their connexion with the personal working of the Spirit. Accord-
1 Pet. i. 2.   ingly, " in the sanctification of the Spirit," that is to say in His whole work of our separation to God, we were by Him at
John xvi. 8.   first brought through conviction
1 Pet. i. 2.   " unto obedience to, and blood-sprinkling of, Jesus Christ." And when the

---

[1] See further below, p. 74.

last step of the blessed process shall come,
and we shall rise transfigured from the grave,
possessing "the adoption, to wit <small>Rom. viii. 23.</small>
the redemption of our body," it will still and
for ever be "because of the Spirit <small>Rom. viii. 11.</small>
who dwelleth in us." Between this Alpha
and this Omega of our personal salvation all
is of "the same Spirit." Does the peaceful
power of grace pervade our regenerate being,
and claim effectually for our Lord all we are
and all we have, and bring spirit, soul, and
body into a delightful captivity and bondservice
to our Head and Possessor? It is <small>Eph. v. 18.</small>
"the fulness of the Spirit." Do we day by
day "mortify the deeds of the body"? It is
"by the Spirit." Do we in truth <small>Rom. viii. 13.</small>
breathe "the Abba, that prayer of faith alone"?
It is the Spirit, the Spirit of adoption, the
Spirit of God's Son in our hearts. <small>Rom. viii. 15, 17.</small>
Do we pray in truth the prayer of <small>Gal. iv. 6.</small>
holy faith and love, the prayer that asks according to His will? It is "in the <small>Jude 20.</small>
Holy Ghost" it is "the Spirit making inter-
cession for us with groanings that <small>Rom. viii. 26.</small>
cannot be uttered." Do "we wait by faith for

the hope of righteousness," the glory reserved
Gal. v. 5.   for the justified? It is "by the
Spirit." Does "Christ dwell in our hearts by
faith?" It is because the Spirit has "strength-
Eph. iii. 16.   ened us with might in our inner man.'

Am I needlessly dwelling upon truths which
are, thanks be to God, our most familiar friends
among the treasures of the Gospel? It is not
wholly for argument that I do so. To me
there seems to lie in the very recitation of our
creed of the Hidden Life a charm and power
which the Spirit Himself can wonderfully em-
ploy to revive or to develop in the soul the
realization and the use of the precious things
which are in some respects so familiar.

But I come now to what was my main
reason for this review of some of the blessings
given us by the Lord the Life-Giver. I come
to say something of the Place of Christ in the
Spirit's work.

And here for the present I will speak not
only briefly but in one direction alone. I will
not dwell upon the all-beloved truth of the
propitiating Cross, and upon the Spirit's witness
to it in our awakened hearts. I will not dwel

at all indeed upon the Spirit's *witness* to the
Lord Jesus. I look at present in the direction
only of our UNION with Jesus Christ in new
birth and life by the Spirit.

The Spirit, as our Communion Creed con-
fesses, is the Life-Giver, the Maker-alive.[1]
But what is the LIFE which He gives, with
which He works? I listen, and I hear another
Voice, which is yet as if also His; John xi. 25;
and it says, "I am the Life." xiv. 6.
"The Life Eternal is in the Son;" "He
that hath the Son hath the Life." 1 John v. 12.
I read these great, these blessed words in
the light of what we have recollected now of
the Holy Spirit's work on and in the Holy Son
of Man; and I thus see in them a remembrance
that what the Spirit does in His free and all-
powerful work in the soul which He quickens
into second life is, above all things, to bring
it into contact with the Son. He roots it, He
grafts it, He embodies it, into the Son. He
deals so with it that there is a continuity wholly
spiritual indeed but none the less most real,

---

[1] Τὸ Ζωοποιόν.

unfigurative, and efficacious, between the Head and the limb, between the branch and the Root. He effects an influx into the regenerate man of the blessed virtues of the nature of the Second Adam, an infusion of the exalted life of Jesus Christ, through an open duct, living, and divine, into the man who is born again into Him the incarnate and glorified Son of God. I see on the one hand the blessed Spirit poured without measure upon the Head. I see Him on the other hand, not independently of that Head but in deepest relation to Him and union with Him, pouring Himself richly into the member. I see Him the divine Factor in the becoming and being of the Manhood of the Second Adam. I see Him equally the divine Factor in the new creation of the sinner into a true child of God, a true regenerate member of the new race. And all this combines to remind me that the blessed process all the while has Jesus Christ for its inmost Secret. What does the Holy Life-Giver impart, infuse, develop? What is my Life Eternal in the last analysis? Not Himself, the blessed Worker and Conveyer, but my incarnate, sacrificed, and

glorified Redeemer and Head.   The Spirit
pours into me HIM, to be my Eternal Life for
deliverance, for victory, for peace, for service,
as truly as He the same Saviour is my pardon and righteousness in His once-wrought
propitiation.

The Life-Giver is the Giver of Christ who
is our Life.

> " Deep through the springs of mind and soul
> Thee the great Comforter inspires;
> Thy sovereign thoughts our thoughts control,
> Thy love our love divinely fires."

We live in a time when every fundamental of
the old and blessed Gospel is too often denied,
or disparaged, or minimized, even by commissioned ministers of the Word, in favour of
something alleged to be more large, and loving
and living.   Let us not be moved.   Let us not
" drift away " with the stream.   Let   Heb. ii. 1.
us not, for lack of taking heed, for lack,
above all, of taking heed in secret *for ourselves*, go away with the multitude. John vi. 66, 67.
But meanwhile let our steadfastness and per-
sistence manifest itself never in *mere* negatives

of rebuke or caution, but more and more in the presentation of our glorious positive. In the tranquil power of the Giver of light and life let us evermore bring into our faith and into our teaching that blessed fulness of the truth as it is in Jesus which is nowhere found more certainly than when we view in their harmony, and use them as we view them, those twin treasures of the old unique Gospel —the saving work of Him who is the one Life, and the saving work of Him who is the one Life-Giver.

CHAPTER III.

THUS far we have dealt almost exclusively with the revealed truth of the Blessed Spirit's personality and divine glory, only turning aside to remember that most sacred and wonderful of all His works, His action in the Incarnation of the Lord Jesus Christ and in the Human Life of the Incarnate One. I do not attempt to retrace any of these steps in the present chapter. Only let me again claim for that last aspect of the doctrine of the Spirit the most earnest, reverent, loving attention of the believer, as he " lives by faith Gal. ii. 20. in the Son of God." A great wealth of spiritual blessing surely lies ready for use, for the Christian who will recollect it and use it, in the truth of the Spirit's work for, on, and in, the Incarnate Lord. That work, that unspeakably deep and precious connexion of the Spirit

with the Redeemer in the work of redemption, is meant to throw the full light of life
eternal upon *our* connexion by the Spirit with
Christ Jesus, who is our Life.   We shall recur
often to this side of truth in later pages ; but
let it be kept always in view.   We, every one
of us who believe on the name of the Son of
1 Cor. vi. 17.   God, are "joined unto Him, one
Spirit."   Our contact, our union, our embodi-
ment, is such as to be rightly described in the
holy Word by that surprising phrase.   And
is not light thrown upon the phrase by the
remembrance that the Spirit who has given
us our Life, who has imparted to us Christ,
is indeed the Spirit of Christ, not only in the
inner relations of Deity, but in the blessed
Incarnation of our glorious Head ?   He who
is Himself thus doubly united to Christ—if I
may express it so—can He not indeed with
richest and holiest fulness pour into us Christ's
members the power and virtues of our Head ?
Indeed He can.   And we therefore, the
favoured members, will bear that fact in wonder-
ing and loving memory.   We will cherish it in
our heart of hearts.   We will use it in our hourly

life. Having the Spirit, we will remember how fully and truly by the Spirit we possess the Son. And in weakness, in sadness, in temptation, under the burthening sense it may be of spiritual decline, we will without delay or misgiving *use* our wonderful treasure. We will by the Spirit *enjoy* our possession of the Son, not after the hour of need but in it. With such a Bond to such a Head, why should we for one minute walk in failure? Nay, "when we are weak, then are we strong;" "in the name of the Lord Jesus, and by 2 Cor. xii. 10. the Spirit of our God." [1] 1 Cor. vi. 11.

And now to advance more directly to the study of the work of the Holy Spirit " for us men and our salvation." And do Thou, most blessed Spirit of God, shine on us and in us as we go!

---

[1] I would earnestly commend to my readers Marshall's *Gospel Mystery of Sanctification* (first published about 1680). It is very old-fashioned, and by no means light reading; but it is full of truth inestimably precious to those who seek to walk with God at once in humble watchfulness and holy liberty. See further p. 174.

It might seem right that we should here
first consider His divine work in creation, in
the " old creation," in " nature." For in a large
range of Scripture passages, from Gen. i. 2
onwards, we find Him mysteriously but dis-
tinctly revealed as the immediate divine Agent
in the making and manipulation, so to speak,
of material things.

But our proposed subject (p. 1) is the
Spirit's work *in redemption*, a subject which
indeed will give us material enough. All I
would do here is to call attention in a general
way to this Scriptural connexion of the SPIRIT
with the world of Matter. It is one among
the many suggestions in the divine Word that
matter has for its immediate basis the absolutely immaterial will and power of God ; that
in this respect, as in others, *la dernière raison
des choses, c'est Dieu.*[1] And, like all those other
suggestions, it reminds the believer, as he rests
on his God for *spiritual* life and power, that
the whole *material* universe, wrought by the

---

[1] Pascal. For a good account of pagan, apocryphal, and
Scriptural views of matter see the note (by Dr F. W. Farrar)
on Wisdom xi. 17 in the *Speaker's Commentary.*

same will that saves him, is infinitely pliable in its Maker's hands for the ultimate good of His spiritual new creation.

Reverently leaving alone, then, this field of truth I turn deliberately to another for some brief but earnest recollections and suggestions. That other field is the *work of the Holy Spirit in relation to the Holy Scriptures.*

I hardly need say that I am aware of the present gravity of that subject, and of the extreme difficulty of speaking upon it to edification amidst the unsettlement, and indeed tumult, of present speculations and negations. But it may be both possible and helpful to take it up in this chapter along a line single, in a sense simple, and yet all-important. We will adhere strictly to the terms of our great subject —the Holy Spirit's work in relation to the Scriptures. It appears to me that many widely prevalent present views of the nature and function of the written Word, however much truth of detail may enter into their formation, err in their *ensemble* by their deeply humanitarian, naturalistic character. Taking up the perfectly true position that human agency and natural .

process are largely present as factors in the
production of Scripture, many an able theorist
declines, or however fails, to see that nevertheless the resultant of the factors of production is not humanitarian, nor naturalistic,
but the divine Word, the supernatural Oracle.
All this failure is the effect far less of a
patient and inductive study of the phenomena
than of the general influence of the modern
tendency to simplify and unify phenomena
under laws as general as possible. It comes
not a little of an instinctive wish to see a
likeness, a homogeneity, and ultimately a oneness, under all spiritual operations and experiences. And so the "inspiration" of Prophet
and Apostle is classified as the same in *genus*,
and even in *species*, as the "inspiration" of the
Christian believer of our day in his walk of faith
and obedience; as a development—in some
respects very high, no doubt, but still only a
development—of the general "consciousness"
of the Church and its members. Isaiah, or the
Isaiahs, and St Paul, were inspired undoubt-
edly; but so, and in essentially the same
way, were Augustine and Anselm, Tauler and

Savonarola, Luther and Bunyan, Oberlin and Elizabeth Fry, nay Plato and Virgil, Shakespeare and Wordsworth, nay the earnest explorer of the structure and processes of material nature, or of the human spirit, or of the written products of that spirit, in whatever region, "secular" or "sacred," human or divine. To all Christian minds and lives, indeed to all grave and elevated minds and lives, Christian or not, some fragments of eternal verities have been somehow disclosed. These they have rendered into word, or act, or both, not always exactly, not always truly, perhaps not always even truthfully, but still so as to give some hints and "broken lights" of the eternal archetype and original. To the devout men who produced the Biblical Literature such disclosures were made in a very remarkable degree, and Scripture accordingly gives us hints of archetypal and eternal truths in a very remarkable way. But to them, as to others, those hints were conveyed only *naturally*, through their moral nature, through experience and reflexion. And so in order to gather up these hints given in the Bible we

4

have to

> " look
> Wisely upon it, as another book." [1]

We have to get the gold of eternal Truth out of the rock of an indefinite amount of human prejudice, mistake, and partial points of view on the part of the human reporters of the truth We are to expect more gold, no doubt, from quarrying the Psalms, and the Gospels, and the Epistles than from quarrying the *Phædo*, or the *Divina Commedia*, or the *Pilgrim's Progress.* But we dig our shaft and sift our diggings in precisely the same way in all the cases.

I am very well aware with what mental energy and skill, and along with what a range and depth of various knowledge, such theories

---

[1] " ' And now,' he cried, ' I shall be pleased to get
  ' Beyond the Bible—there I puzzle yet.'

  " He spoke abash'd—' Nay, nay ! ' the friend replied,
  ' You need not lay the good old book aside ;
  ' Antique and curious, I myself indeed
  ' Read it at times, but as a man should read ;
  ' A fine old work it is, and I protest
  ' I hate to hear it treated as a jest ;
  ' The book has wisdom in it, if you look
  ' Wisely upon it, as another book.' "
  CRABBE, *Tale* xxi., *The Learned Boy.*

in many instances have been constructed and propagated—I hardly need say now "defended," so vast a currency have they obtained. Comparatively few and far between are the modern literary theologians who quite definitely and unmistakably hold that the Holy Scriptures are truly and properly *sui generis* among books as being (as well as containing) the Word of God,[1] and as carrying in a way quite of their own that precious thing, DIVINE AUTHORITY. But I also recollect that in many a past period and crisis the deep tide of intellectual consciousness has taken directions which, on the whole, needed afterwards to be reversed, on a fuller discovery or more calm and reverent review of great facts which had remained all the while unaltered. And I humbly believe that the day will come when the intellectual consciousness of Biblical scientific students as a class will be vastly more alive than it is now to the superhuman and authoritative aspect of the Holy Bible and to the immense significance of that aspect. And such a change of general mental

---

[1] Some weighty words on this subject will be found in Bp Ellicott's recent little volume, *Salutary Doctrine*.

attitude will vastly modify many present theories
about the construction of the Bible, theories
built much less than is sometimes thought upon
the whole facts.

What I attempt to do here is simply to recall
my reader's attention earnestly, gravely, and
with deep conviction to the witness which
the Holy Scripture bears to its own unique
character among books as the Book whose
Author is none other than the Third Person of
the Blessed Trinity. And need I say that this
is no argument in a circle? I ask the Bible
to witness to the Bible ; but I ask the Bible as
literature, as history, to witness to the Bible
as revelation, oracular, authoritative, divine. As
history, capable of verification, it shows me Jesus
Christ, God and Man, living, dying, rising,
proving Himself to be profoundly, ultimately,
trustworthy. But this Jesus Christ, as presented
in the same historical mirror, is seen laying one
hand upon the Prophets and the other upon the
Apostles, and bidding His followers regard with
an altogether unique attention their uttered
messages. And I attend accordingly to those
messages. And in them I find disclosures and

intimations as to the quality and authority of the Biblical writings as the oracles of God which, if words have meaning, put those writings—as to their total character—on a level different in kind from all other literature. I find nothing to forbid me to ask, with deep reverence, whether human personality and natural process were not factors to the product ; and I assuredly find that they were. But I find it emphasized with vastly greater earnestness and fulness that so did the other factor of ultimate divine Authorship govern and manipulate the lower factor that the true Designer and Architect of the Book has *had His way* all along, in the total and in the details too.

I find nothing to enable me to define, in any full or exhaustive way most certainly, the *mode* of the supreme Author's management of the subordinate authors. I find nothing to tell me " what it felt like to be inspired." In many and many a case, I can well believe, it "felt like"—nothing ; nothing distinguishable from other things. I can well believe that when St Paul wrote to Philemon he " felt " nothing supernatural, any more than when Luther wrote to Melanchthon, or Newton to Cowper. *I do not say that it was so;* but it may have been so, for all that we are told. On the other hand I not only can believe, but am sure, that Daniel and St John received their revelations in a state manifestly and entirely abnormal, as Abraham and Moses on certain occasions had done before them ; unless we are to put quietly aside the profoundly solemn assertions to this effect made in Scripture as if they were so much poetical and imaginative excrescence, or framework, because there is so little in human experience outside Scripture, outside this Record of the divine Redemption of fallen man, to verify them. Yes, it is impossible to define or describe Scriptural inspiration as a subjective experience. The *mode*, as to any general account of it, is unknown. " Our theory is not to have a theory." But I do find abundant testimony on the historic surface of the New Testament Scriptures for the strong and unalterable conviction, sure as the historical reality of Jesus Christ our Lord, that a humanitarian, naturalistic view of Scripture is wholly and gravely inadequate to meet the mysterious facts.

I find our Lord and Master Himself handling
the Old Testament Scriptures with the manner
of One who not only owns their general significance but personally cherishes, I dare to say
reveres, their *authority*, even in details of
expression ; and I find Him doing this not only
in the early stages of His course but even more
in the latter, in the last. And I see Him doing
it nowhere more fully and unreservedly than
. when He has overcome death, and   Luke xxiv.
come back from the Unseen in the power of
endless life. And when, exalted into heaven,
He "sends" the blessed Paraclete, His own
promised Representative, the Spirit of Truth, I
find that one main result of the glorious emis-
sion was the incessant use by the Apostles of the
writings of the Prophets, in precisely the spirit,
no less and no more, of their Master before
them.

And I observe one remarkable phenomenon
of the whole case. I find that the Lord and
the Apostles make comparatively little, if I
may reverently say so, of the sacred *writers*
of the Old Testament and comparatively everything of the sacred *writings.* They dwell not

so much on *who said it* as on *what is written.*
No grades of authority appear in their estimate.
What stands within the scrolls of what we
familiarly call the Old Testament, and what He
called the Law, the Prophets, and the Psalms,
is in the eyes of Jesus Christ His Father's
Word, whatever else it is.   As such it is His
weapon in the Temptation, His credential on
the Mount of the Sermon, His mysterious
solace in the Garden,˙ His death-word on the
Cross, His theme upon the Emmaus Road on the
Easter afternoon and in the Upper Chamber
where He stood that evening in His immor-
tality.   Oh blessed road and blessed chamber!
Let us often take our Bibles out with us on
the one, up with us to the other.   We shall
be the less likely then to think that to "look
on the Bible as on another book" is to look
upon it "wisely," even from the point of
view of the strictest induction of truth from
facts.

But now all this mysterious Divinity of the
Bible, this properly miraculous character of it,
this nature of it so entirely refusing to be
accounted for by natural process and human

consciousness, is assigned by itself not to God in general only, but to the HOLY SPIRIT in particular. This is our immediate concern in this enquiry. The statement of the fact is almost all the treatment I give to it ; but what a fact it is to state!

He who was the divine Agent in the blessed Incarnation, He who made and sustained the Manhood of the Second Adam, adjusting it with infinite skill to the blessed Filial Godhead, it is He who was the divine Agent in this glorious parallel process, the construction of Scripture. He, the all-blessed Spirit, in that double union of His with Christ of which we spoke above, so managed the long antecedent march of prophecy, both its substance and its phraseology, that Moses, whatever was the Prophet's "consciousness" in writing, wrote John v. 46, 47. of Christ, and " David in the Spirit " Matt. xxii. 43. called Him his Master, and Isaiah John xii. 39-41. saw His glory and spake of Him ; yes, so that the risen Redeemer Himself found "*in all the Scriptures* the things concerning Himself." So did He design, mani- Luke xxiv. 27. pulate, and accomplish, that " every Scripture

hath in it the Spirit of God." [1] 2 Tim. iii. 16.
So did He fashion "the Word" that it is
"the Sword of the Spirit." So did Eph. vi. 17.
He speak by the Prophets that when an apostolic Writer quotes the words of Heb. x. 15-17.
Jeremiah he ignores, as it were, the Prophet's
personality, intense, tender, and profoundly
interesting and instructive as that particular
personality was. *Majoribus intentus est;* he
is aiming deeper. He is citing the words
as capable of carrying authoritative, decisive
weight on eternal principles and facts. And
he sees nothing for that purpose but their
ultimate Authorship : "Whereof THE HOLY
GHOST also is a Witness unto us ; for after that
He had said before, This is the covenant that
I will make with them after those days, saith
the Lord : I will put My laws into their hearts,
and in their minds will I write them, [then said
He,] And their sins and their iniquities will
Jer. xxxi. 33, 34. I remember no more." The words
are, in a sense, in a true sense, Jeremiah's.

---

[1] The rendering, "Every Scripture inspired of God *is also
profitable*," is not demanded by the Greek. Compare the Greek
of 1 Tim. iv. 4.

But for the Writer to the Hebrews they are simply the words of the Holy Ghost. And so they must be to us, let me add, if we would lean the whole weight of our human need on them in life and in the hour of death. Evacuate Scripture of its divine authority, and you so far paralyse its power for divine consolation.

I thus state something of the outline of the revealed facts of this great and inestimably precious work of the Holy Spirit. I well know that it is but a fragment; it is but a suggestion; it is, in some of its parts, little more than a confession of faith, and a confession of a kind not always very easy to make at the present time. But such as it is I make it to my reader as in the presence of our Lord and Master. At this period in the history of the Church, if I mistake not, it is important in the highest degree to hold fast, and to hold in the foreground of our convictions and our consciousness, the supernatural, the miraculous, the divinely authoritative, aspect of the Holy Scriptures, as the work throughout of none other than the Holy Spirit of God, the blessed Lord of truth and light.

That conviction leaves me, as I have said,

free to enquire into the mode and the materials of the construction of the Scriptural books by their human sub-authors; but with one important exception. It does not leave me free, as I believe, to entertain the theory that any book of the holy Canon, being as to its ultimate authorship the work of the Spirit of Truth, was, from the side of its human authorship, a late fabrication, whose writer sought to borrow an illegitimate prestige by the use of a venerated name and an immemorial date, other than his own.[1]

In conclusion, if indeed the Holy Book is thus the work and word of the Holy Spirit, we have good cause to turn with humble and glad expectation to that Spirit, who dwells in

---

[1] I take occasion to direct the reader's attention to the late Lord Hatherley's *Continuity of Scripture,* to the Rev. C. H. Waller's *Authoritative Inspiration of Scripture,* and to the Rev. A. Cave's recent Congregational Union Lectures on the *Inspiration of the Old Testament.* See also a recent sermon by Dr Liddon, *The Worth of the Old Testament.*

It is scarcely needful to point out that the later "editing" (I use the *term* under some protest) traceable in many passages is a quite different thing from fabrication. The Book of Ecclesiastes *may* have undergone considerable linguistic editing, and yet be no fabrication.

Christ and in us, to open up to the inmost soul as we read it the things of Christ which, according to Christ, are in it everywhere.

Let me quote a few sentences from that grand and "Fruitful Exhortation to the Reading and Knowledge of Holy Scripture," our First Homily of the First Book, and so conclude :—

"The Scripture is full as well of low valleys, plain ways, and easy for every man to use and to walk in, as also of high hills and mountains, which few men can climb unto. And 'whosoever giveth his mind to Holy Scripture with diligent study and burning desire, it cannot be,' saith St John Chrysostom, 'that he should be left without help. For either God Almighty will send him some godly doctor to teach him, . . . or else, if we lack a learned man to instruct and teach us, yet God Himself from above will give light unto our minds, and teach us those things which are necessary for us, and wherein we be igno-rant.' And in another place Chrysostom saith that 'man's human and worldly wisdom needeth not to the understanding of Scripture, but the revelation of the Holy Ghost, who inspireth the true meaning unto them that with humility and diligence do search therefor.' "

" Here is the cause of all our evils," says the same Chrysostom,[1] " our   not *Hom.* ix. *in Col.* knowing the Scriptures."

---

[1] Τοῦτο πάντων αἴτιον τῶν κακῶν, τὸ μὴ εἰδέναι τὰς γραφάς.   This is but a specimen of the language about Scripture used by the Fathers of the first centuries. And yet their age was an age of seething speculation and discussion. They would scarcely have endorsed what has been recently said (not by a Romanist), " The Bible is the most dangerous of God's gifts to man."

CHAPTER IV.

THE previous three chapters are in some measure introductory only. Let us proceed now to the more detailed study of our sacred subject, by the method, at once the simplest and the surest, of taking up some of the great passages of Scriptural revelation and discourse upon it and listening anew to their message in reverent, believing meditation. And as we do so we will remember that the blessed Spirit is not only the true Author of the written Word but also its supreme and true Expositor. Not all my readers know the noble hymn,[1] found in few modern collections, strange to say, in which Cowper has set this forth; and I quote it accordingly in full :—

---

[1] *Olney Hymns,* bk ii., No. 62.

"The Spirit breathes upon the word,
      And brings the truth to sight:
Precepts and promises afford
      A sanctifying light.

" A glory gilds the sacred page
      Majestic, like the sun ;
It gives a light to every age ;
      It gives, but borrows none.

"The hand that gave it still supplies
      The gracious light and heat ;
His truths upon the nations rise ;
      They rise, but never set.

" Let everlasting thanks be Thine,
      · For such a bright display
As makes a world of darkness shine
      With beams of heavenly day.

" My soul rejoices to pursue
      The steps of Him I love,
Till glory breaks upon my view
      In brighter worlds above."

It is true ; we need the Author to be also, in
the inmost secret of the matter, the Expositor,
the Interpreter.   Then will the Written Word
shine, like the Living Word, with the light as
of a transfiguration, its countenance and its
garments also.   Then shall we trace all through
the holy pages "the steps of Him we love," of

Him who has Himself assured us Luke xxiv. 25, that they are to be found there. 27, 44, 45. John v. 39.

It may be well here, however, to say one word of caution as to the use made by the Christian of this truth of the Spirit's expository work. *How* may we expect Him normally to exercise for us this merciful function ? Is it by direct illumination, such that this text or that passage shall be seen by the soul, in the way of supernatural intuition, to mean this or that ? If I am not mistaken, this impression is widely spread among Christians ; and I would not lightly or without sympathy speak in correction of it. Nevertheless it must be obvious, on reflection, that to expect the Holy One to act upon us in such a manner as this is to expect the gift, just so far as such action goes, of prophetic infallibility. It makes my interpretation, arrived at under such illumination, as truly a divine revelation as the text itself, and it precludes any criticism of my interpretation, because it thus is, at least in essentials, the interpretation of God. When I hear or read, as I sometimes do, that a Christian believer speaks of this or of that as having been "shown

5

to him " in such and such a text, I am well
aware that the meaning of the phrase, as the
speaker intends it, *may* be most true, healthful,
and trustworthy. But it is also possible that it
may involve a claim, a dangerous claim, to hold
and teach the interpretation in question as one
above examination, because inspired, because
divinely intuitive. What then are we to think
of the matter ? Are we, after all, to apply ourselves to Scripture study without special prayer
and special expectation ? Are we to assume
practically that " the natural man *doth* receive
See 1 Cor. ii. 14. the things of the Spirit of God ; "
that they are *not* " foolishness unto him ; " that
they are not, necessarily and only, " spiritually
discerned " ? Shall we, after all, in face of all
that we recollected in the previous chapter, think
that to look on the Bible as on " another book "
is to look upon it " wisely " ? No ; the mistake
of doing so is not only great but fatal in our
Scripture study, and we will not make it. We
clergy at least, in the words of our Second
Ordination Service, "will continually pray to
God the Father, through the mediation of
our only Saviour Jesus Christ, for the heavenly

assistance of the Holy Ghost, that by daily
reading and weighing of the Scriptures we may
wax riper and stronger in our ministry." And
what the clergyman thus does in view of his
special function, the private Christian will do in
view of his, in view of his sacred " ministry,"
his " work of ministry,"[1] his whole   Eph. iv. 12.
life as laid at the Lord's feet for His use.
But the point is this. We shall ask, not for
mental infallibility, which is asking in effect
for a gift that has been " annulled,"   1 Cor. xiii. 8.
but for spiritual submission, receptivity, and
harmony with the Spirit of God, such that
our reverent inquiry into the meaning of the
Spirit's words may be carried on   1 Cor. ii. 13.
in spiritually "dry light." We shall pray for
such presence and power of the Holy One
within us, at the " springs of thought and will,"
that we may be *morally* ready for the least hint,
the tenderest suggestion, given in the blessed
Book, about the will and mind of the author of
the Book. Such a prayer will on the one hand
recognize at every step our helplessness where

---

[1] Διακονια : see the construction of the Greek sentence.

we really are helpless. It will on the other
hand only quicken us in the diligent and patient
work of attention, and research, and comparison,
as we use that precious mental faculty which
the Lord who made us, and remade us, has
given us to be used as in His presence and
for Him. And the result will be no mere
prolonged uncertainty, as if we were perpetually
in fear lest new Scriptural evidence should
upset our deepest spiritual certainties. By the
grace of God it will be a calm and settled
certainty, solid yet developing, the resultant of
spiritual simplicity and of the genuine mental
discovery and acquisition which such simplicity
powerfully assists. It will be a certainty, as
to all things of salvation, practically absolute
to ourselves. But it will be kept clear of all
untenable claims to have *prophetic authority
over others.*[1]

---

[1] I may refer the student to an excellent passage on this
subject in an excellent book, the late Mr G. Stanley Faber's
Primitive Doctrine of Justification, pp. 233, etc. (ed. 1839).
Mr Faber is dealing with Bishop Bull's peculiar theory of Justification by Faith, a theory as to which the Bishop says that he
attained to a firm persuasion of its truth after earnest prayer for
mental illumination.

I have digressed at some length. And I would close my digression with an appeal, all the more earnest after the cautions on which I have ventured, to make the closing verses of 1 Cor. ii., after all, one of our ruling mottoes for all study of the Word of God.

Approaching now some of the great Scriptural passages which discourse of the Holy Spirit and His work, I observe that these are to be found, in the main, in the writings of St John and of St Paul. I propose then to take some such passages from each of these Apostles in turn, and to examine their witness, with a special view always to the spiritual life of myself and of my reader. St Paul's writings will afford us several such passages, mainly from the Roman, Corinthian, Galatian, and Ephesian Epistles. In St John's Gospel we have, above all things, the precious Discourse of the Upper Chamber, but also _{John xiv.-xvi.} passages in the third, seventh, and twentieth chapters. In the First Epistle we have much incidental material. In the Revelation the blessed Spirit appears again and again, and in connexions full of doctrinal and spiritual teaching.

Let us take St John's Gospel first, both because it comes first in the Canon, and because in it, with scarcely any exception, the teaching about the Spirit comes from the very lips of the Son. The passage of passages here is the Paschal Discourse. But some shorter while all-important, passages precede it, which we now take up, for brief but most reverent meditation on their divine instruction.

The first passage, the only one I can touch John iii. 1-8. at present, is the first part of the conversation with Nicodemus.

How shall I deal with it? First, necessarily, by excluding from the inquiry many extremely interesting subsidiary points. I do not forget, but I must not now consider, the connecting "but," or "now"[1] (unaccountably omitted by the Authorized Version), which links the passage to the statements just before. I do not forget, but I must now pass by, the question what precise motive brought Nicodemus to the

---

[1] Ἦν δὲ ἄνθρωπος, κτλ.

Lord, and what led the Lord to speak instantly
to him about the *kingdom* and entrance into it.
And indeed I do not forget the weighty importance of the passage in the study of the
doctrine of Christian Baptism, to which I cannot
doubt reference is made in the word   John iii. 5.
" water," though I know that much has been
thoughtfully said on the other side.   But I do
not dwell upon this now.   Not that I undervalue
the momentousness of the question raised ; not
that I regard the divine Sacrament with feelings
other than humble reverence and thankfulness.
But I believe that the passage contains elements
of truth which have usually received far less
attention, certainly in current thought in the
Church at large, than the baptismal reference
has received, and which yet have the most
important bearing on that reference, such that
they should help to interpret it rather than it
claim to explain them.   And these elements I
find above all in ver. 8 : " The wind bloweth
where it listeth, and thou hearest the sound
thereof, but canst not tell whence it cometh,
and whither it goeth ; so is every one that is
born of the Spirit." " Ye must be born again."

Take this sacred utterance up in detail.

1. " BORN of the Spirit." Read the phrase as if new, as if in a recently discovered document of the first century. How powerful the term is, how profound! The word is not merely altered, influenced, reformed, reinvigorated. It is born, born again, born from above, touched with a *biogenesis* which is indeed the impartation of a higher order of life,[1] for it is Life Eternal. The man is taken back to a new beginning, set going again under new provisions and conditions of life, stamped with a new spiritual impression,[2] the living family likeness of the sons of God. Would we estimate the weight and fulness of what is meant by this wonderful phrase ? Then let us take the New Testament, and examine again, under the Spirit's illumination on our spirits, all the many passages where "childhood" and "sonship" of the

E.g. Rom. viii., 1 John iii., v., etc.

---

[1] Readers of *Natural Law in the Spiritual World* will recognize my allusion to the first chapter of that book. I cannot go with all Professor Drummond's contentions in the book, believing that he not seldom sees identities where analogies would be a truer word. But the lessons and suggestions of the first chapter seem to me very valuable indeed.

[2] Χαρακτήρ.

spiritual kind are spoken of; the places which
direct us how to know the "children of God,"
what are their notes and marks, what are
their characteristic thoughts of God, of Christ,
of the brethren of Christ, what, in short, they
are, and what they *do*, as "the sons and
daughters of the Lord Almighty." 2 Cor. vi. 18.
"Whatsoever is born of God overcometh the
world;" "As many as are led by the Spirit
of God, they are the sons of God;" "Behold,
what manner of love, that we should be called
the sons of God.   Therefore the world knoweth
us not, because it knew Him not."   These are
celestial words, penetrating and searching the
soul.   Well may St Augustine say,[1] "Let all
sign themselves with the Cross, let all say the
Amen and the Hallelujah, let all be baptized,
let all enter the church doors; the children of
God are distinguished from the children of the
devil only by love. They who have love are
born of God; they who have not love are
not."[2]

---

[1] On 1 John v. 7.

[2] I venture to refer the reader to a little treatise of my own,
The New Birth.

2. "Born of THE SPIRIT." To Him, the
blessed Third Person, the sacred Subject of our
studies, the Lord Jesus Christ here assigns the
immediate agency in the New Birth. HE takes
in hand the man, and deals with him in regenerating efficacy. He conveys to him the eternal
life whose secret and at the same time whose
manifestation is love generated of the love of
God. He ploughs the ground of the soul,
convincing it of sin, righteousness, and judgment. He inserts the vivifying seed, so that
1 Pet. i. 23. the man is "born again by the word
of God, which liveth and abideth for ever."
Rom. v. 5. He "pours out the love of God in
the heart." He both gives the child-state and
Rom. viii. 15. teaches the new-born man to under-
Gal. iv. 6. stand it, to cry "Abba Father,"
"the Abba, that prayer of faith alone,"[1] to
the Eternal and Invisible.

3. "So is every one that is born of the
Spirit." We come last to the first word of
this divine sentence : "So." Of the "men," of
the human beings, thus born again, born of the

---

[1] Paul Gerhardt's *Song in the Day of the East Wind.*

Spirit, a certain something is universally, is at the very least normally, true ; true not of some of them, not of a kind or class among them, but of "every one." Οὕτως ἐστὶ πᾶς ὁ γεγεννημένος ἐκ τοῦ Πνεύματος.

The reference of "so" is clear, is unmistakable. The Lord has just used a familiar but vivid illustration, as was His wont. He has spoken of the breath of air, the "spirit" of material nature, of its mystery and of its evidence. In certain of its phenomena He sees the counterpart of the case of "every one that is born of the Spirit."

And this in three main respects, which I briefly indicate, though perhaps there is slight need that I should do so.

First, there is in the two cases an analogous *secrecy of process*. The breathing atmosphere fans my forehead, plays in the tree above me, whispers in the grass and rushes of the riverside below me. It is in itself meanwhile an infinitely delicate and quite invisible wave or current in the airy ocean ; and all the combined observation and inference of mankind could not tell—certainly I could not tell—where that wave in the pure deep began and where it will sink into repose again. "*So* is every one that is born of the Spirit;" the process is mysterious. The man receives a divine power upon him, within him. He is alive unto God, knowing Him, loving Him, lovingly bent upon pleasing Him "as His own son˙ that serveth Him." And he knows that he did not originate for himself this condition; he did not beget and bear himself again to living hope, to loving life. Perhaps he knows definitely when, in some day or hour of mercy, he was awakened, convinced, enlightened, enabled to give himself to God. But this is but part of the secret, one mighty symptom of the process. He does not know when and how the holy work really began, how long the Spirit, who brought him to the New Birth at last, who was, in Hooker's words[1] "thus effectual in the secret work of regeneration unto newness of life," had been preparing for that bright hour, by secret pleadings, by unnoticed providences, by even slighted means of grace—slighted, yet leaving *some*

Mal. iii. 17.

---

[1] *Serm. i. on Jude* 17-21.

mark on thought and will. He may know when the wind manifestly swayed him ; he does not know whence and how it came on its holy path. And truly he knows not whither it goeth ; " it doth not yet appear what 1 John iii. 2. he shall be."

Secondly, the air-wave illustrates the mystery of the New Birth by its *independence as regards the will of man.* Putting aside exceptions which are altogether trivial, the streams of the vast atmospheric ocean do indeed not obey the will of man. He cannot originate, he cannot steer for one mile, for one yard, the broad current either of the zephyr of the summer evening or of " the storm that wrecks the winter sky." From his point of view "it bloweth where it listeth." Even so the Spirit " distributeth," divideth, giveth, moveth, "as He will." The sons of God are 1 Cor. xii. 1. " born, not of the will of the flesh, nor of the will of man (ἀνήρ), but of God." It John i 13. is a truth never meant to discourage, to repel, to bewilder ; for this sovereignty of will is the sovereignty of Him whose "fruit is Gal. v. 22. love, joy, peace," of Him concerning whom it is

written, "Your heavenly Father shall give His
Holy Spirit to them that ask Him." But it is
Luke xi. 13. a truth meant to humble, meant to
keep us low indeed before the eternal Will.

Thirdly, the New Birth is illustrated by the
action of the wind in respect of *evidence given
in results.* Here is one plain point in our
blessed Lord's parable, all-important, yet often
overlooked. The wave of air, in its origin,
course, and issues, is mysterious, invisible, unde-
finable ; but its presence around me and in my
surroundings is to be known by practical results, and by them alone : "Thou hearest the
sound, the voice." The trees of the wood, the
waters of the mountain lake, you "hear the
wind" in them and on them ; and thus you
ascertain its presence there. "So is every one
that is born of the Spirit ; " every one. The
divinely mysterious process produces known
and observable effects ; and its presence, its
presence not in the abstract but here or there,
is to be verified by them, and by them alone.
Regeneration, the coming to be one of the children of God, in Augustine's sense of that term,
in John the Apostle's sense, in the Lord's sense,

is indeed a " secret thing " in itself ; but its evidences are practical and plain. The Spirit is eternal, divine ; but where He effectually works the New Birth, there, in one degree or another, so says the Lord here, you will hear the sound, you will trace results. And what *is* the sound of the heavenly Wind in the being, in the life ? It consists of things which indeed belong to, though they are not the creatures of, the circumstances of the common day : "love, joy, peace, longsuffering, gentleness, goodness, faith- fulness, meekness, self-control." It Gal. v. 22, 23. consists, in fact, of love, love in distribution, heaven-given love to God and to man in God.

It will be obvious that these remarks have much to do, supposing them to be true, with our interpretation of the function of the blessed Sacrament of Baptism, and in particular of the language of our own baptismal ritual. Into the deeply interesting and important questions so suggested, questions Scriptural, ecclesiastical, historical, questions amongst others of the nature of the absolute language of ceremony as against the more guarded language of bio- graphy, I do not enter here, for I think they

are not in place in these meditations.[1]   Only it
is right that I should say for my own part that
not one word above written has been written
in forgetfulness of my obligations as a presbyter
of the English Church, or with faltering convictions as to the rightness of the language of
its sacramental ritual.   All the more earnestly
would I say, and not least to my brethren
in the ministry of the Word and Sacraments,
Let nothing, absolutely nothing, be allowed to
obscure our sense of the unutterable moral
weight of our Redeemer's words in this great
passage of St John: " Ye must be born again.
So is every one that is born of the Spirit."

William Beveridge, Bishop of St Asaph
(1704—1708), was no half-hearted Churchman.
Among our elder divines few use language
about the holy Sacraments more reverent, I
might say more rapturous, than his.   Let me
close then with a brief extract from his seventy-
third printed sermon[2]: " *Christ's Resurrection
the Cause of our Regeneration:*"—

---

[1] I venture to refer to my *Outlines of Christian Doctrine*,
p. 249, etc.

[2] *Works*, ed. 1824, vol. iv., p. 240.

" By your care and pains about the things of this world you may perhaps get something in it, and perhaps not, and how much so ever it be, it is nothing at all in comparison of what the children of God all have ; ' all things are theirs,' all things that God hath made, and He Himself too that made them. And what can they desire more ? There is nothing more for them to desire ; and therefore their minds must needs be at rest, and their souls as full as they can hold of all true joy and comfort.

" Who then would not be in the number of these blessed souls ? Who would not be regenerate, and made a child of God, if he might ? And who may not, if he will ? Blessed be God, we are all as yet capable of it, for now that Christ is risen from the dead and exalted at the right hand of God, to be a Prince and a Saviour, to give repentance and forgiveness of sins, if we do but apply ourselves to Him and believe and trust on Him for it, His Father will be ours too ; He will beget us again in His own likeness, and admit us into the glorious liberty of His own children."

G

CHAPTER V.

OUR last thoughts were given to the work of the Holy Spirit as He effects the New Birth. We considered Him as He deals with Eph. ii. 1. man "dead in trespasses and sins," and brings him into that wonderful "newness Rom. vi. 4. of life" in which "henceforth" he Gal. v. 25. Rom. viii. 15. is to "walk by the Spirit," possessing "the Spirit of adoption, in whom we cry, Abba, Father."

> "Our quicken'd souls awake and rise
> From the long sleep of death ;
> On heavenly things we fix our eyes,
> And praise employs our breath."

In the present chapter I ask my reader to take a step in some sense backward. In studying the work of Regeneration we also studied, by reason of the spiritual connexion of the two things, some of the phenomena of

Conversion; that wonderful turning about of the inward man which corresponds as nearly as possible in its idea to the great Scripture word Repentance.[1] For let it never be forgotten that Repentance means more, very much more, than regret, or even remorse, or even "godly sorrow."[2] It is a deep, decisive alteration in the attitude of the soul towards God, and His glory, and His claim, and His salvation. "The sinner that repenteth" is the sinner <small>Luke xv. 7-10.</small> that is converted, turned back, brought back from loss to salvation, from the wilderness to the fold, from the far-off land to the Father's home.

This however is by the way. I was recalling the fact that we have already considered some of the main phenomena of that blessed change which is as to its divine secret and agency New Birth, and as to its human experience Conversion. And thus we take in some sort a step backward to consider now the great initial step of that work as wrought by the

---

[1] Μετάνοια.

[2] See 2 Cor. vii. 10 for clear proof of this, in a passage full of instruction on the matter.

Spirit, whether for the world or the soul, that step which is called Conviction of Sin. This line of inquiry, however, will not be retrograde in any unreasonable way. Not seldom a great subject is best studied first by a brief view of its whole, and then by closer attention to its parts. In this chapter and in some subsequent pages we will deal thus with the decisive work of our blessed Life-Giver, looking for His merciful light.

The Scripture which puts prominently forward the convincing work of the Holy Spirit is, I hardly need say, John xvi. 8-11 ; part of that divine Discourse to which we owe, as we have remembered already, our central revelations about the blessed Spirit's Personality, and about very much of His work. The wording of this particular passage calls of course for most careful study. And so I would not fail to notice two leading features of it ; first, that it speaks of the Spirit's convincing work as done in and on " the world," distinguished from the disciples of Jesus ; secondly, that it connects that work in the closest way with the Lord

Jesus Christ Himself :—" because they believe not on Me ;" " because I go to My Father." Nor do I forget that " conviction of *sin* " is only one of three convictions spoken of in the passage ; I do not lose sight of the " righteousness " and the " judgment." But on this latter point it will appear, I think, as we go on that so close is the relation of the two latter convictions to the first, and that they are in some respects so subordinated to the first, that we may venture lawfully to group the whole work under the title of Conviction of Sin.

Now first a few words on the reference or this great work to " *the world,*" that is to the mass of unregenerate humanity. It has been thought by some interpreters that this mention of the world excludes from the passage a distinct reference to the Spirit's saving operation in individual souls. And so the point and bearing of the Saviour's sentences here has been supposed to be directed towards what I may call *public human opinion* about Christ's character and work, and about the momentous awfulness of *sin*, as the great contradiction to *righteousness* (now glorified in Christ), and as

the sure subject of coming *judgment* to be
exercised by Christ, who has already given
earnest of His final exercise of judgeship in
His victory over the world's Prince. In this
view we are to look for the fulfilment and
explanation of the words in such great phenomena as, for instance, the awe which fell
upon the Jews as a nation when the Pentecostal
effusion came and the Gospel work began;
an awe indicated in one way or another all
through the Acts. Or again, to take a yet
larger example, we may look for the fulfilment
in that greatly deepened sense (for such it is)
of the shame of wrong, and the glory of
righteousness, and the depth and solemnity of
coming retribution, which has pervaded mankind as a mass wherever Christianity has been,
even inadequately, proclaimed. And certainly
this is one of the greatest facts of human
history, however it is explained. And to the
believer no explanation of it will be adequate
which does not connect it with the work of the
Holy Spirit upon the human conscience, as He
makes the human soul able to interpret to
itself, however dimly, the moral and spiritual

significance of the Person, Character, and Sacrifice of Jesus Christ. And it is perfectly true that such public, general, universal conviction may, and alas continually does, fall quite short in individuals of the conviction which "worketh repentance unto salvation ;" and that therefore it may be studied as a work which moves out side the inner circles of the Spirit's saving action upon souls ; as a work emphatically in "*the world.*"

But all this says only, at most, that the words of our Master in John xvi. do, or may, refer to a so to speak indefinite and diffused operation of the Spirit, but it does not say that they do not also, and in a special and central degree, refer to His inner circles of effectual blessing. For surely wherever that effectual blessing takes place, wherever a soul in its mysterious individual personality is awakened from the sleep of sin and born of the Spirit, it is a case in which a member of "the world" has been dealt with, in the world, to be brought out of the world. It is a case in which the blessed Agent, like Him whom He glorifies, has gone into the outer wilderness.

and has led from it a rescued wanderer, lately dead in sins, blinded by the god of this world, Eph. ii. 2. "walking according to its course." In this new convert, whether from open heathenism, or heresy, or infidelity, or from a profession of the blessed Faith which is in name only, we find just the general facts of "the world" individualized. Just that which, in a sense less definite and intense, is done by the Spirit for the world as world, is done by the same Spirit in a sense most definite, most effectual, for this member of the world as individual will and soul. He has brought the man to "conviction of sin, righteousness, and judgment," in the light of Christ.

And it is manifest, by the way, that the large, wide, work of conviction in the sphere of general opinion is done in no small measure through these isolated occurrences, these deep, individual convictions of sin. So it has been from the beginning. The thousands of definite convictions, repentances, and baptisms at Pentecost, were a mighty means for diffusing through the Jewish public mind an impression about Christ and the Gospel far short indeed

in itself of regeneration and salvation, yet incal-
culably precious and important. And so it is
to this day. Nothing can more powerfully
contribute to keep up, and to raise up, "the
world's" public consciousness of sin, righteousness, and judgment than the presence in it, as
salt-grains in the mass, of individuals intensely
and savingly convinced of those three things
for themselves, in the light of immediate dealings for themselves with God in Christ. And
nothing would so fatally lower "the world's"
public moral and quasi-Christian consciousness
as that such individual convictions, such personally convinced ones, should become few and
fewer, till religion itself should be dissociated
in common opinion from the very ideas conveyed by the words, "*I* have sinned against
the Lord;" "What must *I* do to be saved?"

So without misgiving I take these words of
the Lord Jesus, and see in them His assurance
that the Holy Spirit, in the Gospel Age, and as
the divine Messenger to souls, and Illuminator
of souls, about Himself the Saviour, should
convince the individual unregenerate heart, in
merciful speciality, of sin, and righteousness, and

judgment. He should "open" it to "attend to"
Acts xvi. 14. its unspeakable *need* of Christ; and
to the *sin* against the love of God, and against
itself, of indifference or refusal in presence
of a manifested Christ; and to the awful
glory of *righteousness*, the eternal antithesis to
all trangression of the law, a glory now trans-
cendently displayed in the exaltation of the
crucified Christ Jesus to the heavens; and to
the ineffable rightness, certainty, and eternity
of the *judicial ruin* of sin and all that sides
with sin—a ruin already in effect accomplished
by the personal triumph of the Son of God
over His mysterious personal Antagonist, the
world's prince and god. So, according to this
passage, should the Spirit of truth, holiness,
and love, deal with the individual. Such
should be the personal conviction of sin, righteousness, and judgment, under His operating
hand. In a way that should make use of all
the moral faculties of the man, and yet should
work from infinitely above them, and penetrate
if it be possible beneath them, He should bring
the inner eyes to see something of the realities
of this great matter, so that the man should

say with the voice of his inmost being, "I have sinned against the Lord and His glorious Christ; what must I do?"

May I make bold to turn to my reader, and laying aside the tone of mere enquiry and discussion, speak to him as to a brother man? I venture to ask you, does this brief, fragmentary indication of the Spirit's sin-convincing work correspond in any degree to your consciousness, to your experience? Ah, surely it does. For indeed such things have been taking place in souls ever since the day when at the great Effusion, *and as its very first result*, three thousand human individuals "were pricked in their heart, and said, Men and brethren, what shall we do?" Paul was convinced _{Acts ii. 37.} of sin, and so was the Philippian Jailer, and so was Augustine, and so was Luther, and so were Hooker, and Pascal, and Bunyan, and Brainerd, and Wesley, and Simeon, and Chalmers,— strange collocation of names, men in almost every respect dissimilar, but alike in this common characteristic of conviction of sin. And who shall count the examples of the same work,

here and now, in our time, in our land, in every
land where the Gospel of the Son of God has
found its way ?   No law of sex, or age, or tem-
perament, or circumstances, can be traced in the
matter ; no law but that "of the Spirit of life in
_{Rom. viii. 2.} Christ Jesus." This convicting whisper
and unveiling finds its way to the youngest and
to the most aged conscience, to the miserable
and to the happy in external conditions, to the
savage and to the scholar, to the profligate and
to the man who on every standard short of that
of God in Christ is, as Saul of Tarsus was,
sincerely moral.   So I count it altogether likely
that my reader is one who can "set to his seal"
that the doctrine of individual conviction of sin
by the Holy Spirit is true, is true for him.   I
do not know, I cannot guess, how it has come
to him ; the manner, and method, and occasion.
Perhaps, as a matter of biography, it has come
not in the first pages of his Christian experience, but later.   So Zinzendorf, whose conversion came in the first phase of it through an
overpowering insight into the love and loveliness of his Redeemer,[1] was taught not till later

---

[1] See further below, p. 112.

the depths of his need of that Redeemer's sacrifice. Perhaps it has come, not as one great critical occasion, one narrow while intense cloud to be passed through, but rather stage by stage, in intervals and developments of self-discovery. Or perhaps—and indeed such cases do take place—it was really the decisive *first* handling of your soul, so far as you can estimate such facts, by the great Regenerator. In some course of open or hidden rebellion against the light, or just in the midst of dull or complacent indifference ; in the house of God, in the mission-hall, amidst many awakened ones, or quite as likely in the walk on the hill-side or in the street, or in your own room at college, or at home ; lo, the Spirit touched you into an insight you had not even imagined before of sin, and righteousness, and judgment ; of the *necessity* and the reality of Christ. And as in that conviction, soon or slowly, you were led by the same blessed Worker up to the point of simplest acceptance of your crucified Lord for your Saviour and your King, you know how the whole colour and texture of subsequent faith was affected through and through by

the initial conviction.　Everything took results
from it.　Your insight into the wonder, glory,
and virtue of the Propitiation ; your submission
Rom. ii. 8.　　to the revealed "indignation and
wrath" of the righteous Judge, and your rejection for ever of the "vain words" which
try to say that that wrath is not actually
Eph. v. 6.　　"coming upon the children of disobedience ;" your pity and love for souls as yet
entranced in the sleep from which you have
been awakened ; all became what they could
not be, could not possibly be, without some
genuine personal experience of the Spirit's
convincing power.

You understood now, in the moral sense of
understanding, what is meant by the remark
that " Christianity cannot be proved except
to a bad conscience."　For " bad " you read
" awakened ; " and it is indeed true for you.
The Gospel is a message not for man in the
abstract, but for man a sinner.　Till you saw
yourself to be this latter, under the Spirit's
convictions, the Gospel was a something for
which you seemed to find in yourself no true
receptacle, a key which did but rattle, so to

speak, in a lock not made exactly for it. Now the Spirit has spoken to your soul of sin ; and with a blessed intuition you behold, and believe, the divine provision for your release alike from its guilt and from its power. " *Rock of Ages* " is a new hymn to the man who is convinced by the Paraclete of sin, righteousness, and judgment. And wonderfully now does the Bible open itself to that man, and fall into order and relation before him, and disclose its inner harmonies in his sight. The Protevan- Gen. iii. 15. gelium of Genesis is no myth to him now, nor are the sacrifices of the Mosaic altar an invention of man. Every type and prophecy is lighted up by its relation to the Cross, and in turn lights up the convinced man's apprehension of the Cross in the holy details of its ever-blessed significance. And precious indeed to him now is every trace of apostolic doctrine which unfolds the treasures of the accomplished mystery of Calvary. The third chapter of the Romans, and of the Galatians, and the whole teaching of the Hebrews, culminating in xiii 20, 21, are dear to him now with a sense of personal companionship and intimacy. So Jesus Crucified,

like the celestial bow upon the cloud, is manifested as God's Antithesis to the manifestation
of the guilt of sin. And so is Jesus Risen
manifested, as He had not been, as He could
not be before, in all the glory of His finished
work, and His indwelling and sin-subduing
Presence (by the same Spirit who has thus
convinced the soul), and in all the warmth and
1 Pet. i. 3. radiance of that "living hope" to
which the man is now personally and indi-
vidually "begotten again." And as this richly
blessed penitent looks forward to the now dear
and happy prospect of the life to come, in the
peace and strength of an evidence of its reality
as real as it is internal, what is his anticipation?
He looks for a world, a life, a work, of sinless
bliss, of entire and positive holiness in everlasting personal joy ; but he looks to live, love,
and *serve* there as one who will for ever rejoice
(wonderful paradox) to remember that "*when
Rom. v. 8. we were sinners, Christ died for
us,*" and to praise the blessed Name not of
an abstract Deity but of "GOD and of THE
Rev. vii. 10. LAMB."

Was it too bold of the medieval believers

to say, " *O beata culfa, quæ talem meruisti Redemptorem;* " " Blessed guilt, which hast won such a Redeemer " ?

We need conviction for ourselves as individuals, if our personal religion is to *strike root downward*, and so to bear fruit upward. The man who knows little of conviction of sin, as a genuine element in personal experience, may be many good things, but I do not think he can be a deep Christian.

And greatly do we pastors need this for our ministry. A full, strong current of opinion in the professing Church of Christ runs at the present day directly against a grave, thoroughgoing, doctrine of sin, and its correlative truths of eternal judgment, and of the unspeakable need of the atoning blood, and of living personal faith in the Crucified and Risen One, " according to the Scriptures." One would think that some even earnest teachers had learned, by some other path surely than that of the Word of God, to look with temperate eyes upon sin, as a phenomenon sure at last to disappear under long processes of divine Order ; a discord awaiting only its musical

7

resolution ; a "fall upward," perhaps, on to
some higher level of enriched consciousness.

Let no man deceive us with vain words.
And let us pray that our lips may never pass
them on. And to that intent may the Holy
Spirit of Promise evermore teach us, close to
the Cross and to the open Grave, His lessons
of sin, of righteousness, and of judgment.

Even so. But from *every other* aspect of
the matter we must say, we must cry, the very
opposite of "*O beata culpa.*" And we who
believe, and who have been convinced of sin,
righteousness, and judgment, must humbly and
persistently look to the same holy Convincer
who began the work that He may deepen it
and develop it throughout our whole lives,
and (let me add to my ministerial brethren)
throughout our whole ministry. If in one
aspect the conviction of sin is the great initial
work of the Spirit, from another aspect it is
a work which we can never dare to wish Him
to wind up here below. Has the believer ever
reached the real end of self-discovery ? Has
he ever really seen with ultimate adequacy
how truly his happiest actual obedience " cannot

endure the severity of the *divine judgment* " ? [1]
Has he ever quite fully realized his need of
" Christ for him " ? No, he has not. So now,
and to-morrow, and always, we will ask the
Convincer to carry on in the blessed home o¹
Grace the lesson He mercifully began upon
the desert sands ; to keep us alive and awake,
tenderly, humbly, and evermore, to sin, and
righteousness, and judgment, in the light, in
the blissful light, of Christ.

---

[1] Article XII. See below, p. 188.

CHAPTER VI.

WE have endeavoured to think out something of the great subject of Conviction of Sin by the Spirit of God. Perhaps I should rather say not to think it out, but to think it in; to turn inward in view of it, and question our souls, writer and reader together, about our _{Rom. vii 13.} own insights into the " exceeding sinfulness of sin" in the light of the Holy Ghost.

I turn now to the glorious other side of the operation of the Spirit in His work of new creation, re-constitution, of us sinners. I turn to His dealings with us in the way of making our Lord Jesus Christ to be to us what He is given to be to such as we are—our spiritual "life, and breath, and all things;" our righteous- _{1 Cor. i. 30.} ness, and sanctification, and redemption"; our joy, our peace, our power, our hope. We have seen the Heavenly Worker ploughing the soil, breaking up the fallow, crushing the underlying rock into dust. We see Him now dropping the seed, letting fall the divine "corn of wheat" into the ground. We John xii. 24. see Him applying Christ to the sorely needing soul, now conscious of its need. And we see Him to this end dealing with it as the Spirit of Manifestation, "revealing in it the Son of God." Gal. i. 16.

Here is indeed the Holy Spirit's congenial, beloved work. For He is the "Spirit of Christ." And in our second chapter we saw how deep the indications of that phrase go; how the Spirit is not only the Emissary of Christ but, in the inner Life of Godhead, the Stream from Him the Fountain. Wonderful is the union of nature and of operation so indicated; wonderful, blissful, divinely deep and tender, the union and communion of that Love of the Spirit and the Son.

Let us dwell a little on this point of truth. It is possible, and it is not uncommon, so to dwell on the convincing work of the Spirit as to associate His action mainly with that side of grace; as if His *characteristic* were to

penetrate, to detect, to expose the soul to
itself, to cast it down wounded and broken.
But no, it is not so.   I have striven to lay
all the emphasis I can on the unspeakable
importance of the work of conviction.   But
therefore I am all the more free to remind
my reader and brother that this is after all
the Spirit's "strange work."   The Eternal
_{Neh. ix. 20.} Dove, the Spirit of grace, the "Good
Spirit," has for His *dear and welcome* function
the uplifting of the sweet glory of Christ to
the aching eyes of the contrite ; the applying
of the soft balm of Christ to the wounds He
Himself has mercifully made through "soul
_{Heb. iv. 12.} and spirit."

There is a delightful little book by the late
venerable Dr Horatius Bonar, *The Gospel of
the Spirit's Love.*   It is only a tract, of less
than fifty pages ;[1] but it is full of that *Theology
of Consolation*[2] which has few better modern
expositors than the deeply taught saints and

---

[1] Edinburgh: A. Stevenson, North Bank Street. 2nd ed.,
1884.

[2] I borrow the phrase from the title of a very valuable
historical doctrinal work by the Rev. D. C. A. Agnew. (Edinburgh: 1881.)

thinkers trained in the thorough views of our sin and ruin expounded in the Scottish Confession, and in that adoring insight into the wonder, and glory, and tenderness of the work of grace which seems specially given to those who have accepted the whole truth of man's ruin. I commend this little book to my reader. It will press home on him on every side the conviction that indeed "Thy Spirit *is* _{Ps. cxliii. 10.} *good*;" that the Love of the Spirit, as truly as that of the Son, "passeth knowledge;" that it is a deep mistake, a fallacy which chills and blights the soul's life, to fail to recognize this; "as if there were something in the Spirit which repelled us, whatever there might be in Christ to attract us; as if the light which the Cross throws upon the love of the Spirit were not quite in harmony with that which it reveals of the love of Christ; as if the Spirit were not always as ready with His help as is the Son" (p. 21). And one passage, close to this short quotation, speaks in words pregnant with truth about our special subject here, His glorification of Christ to us :—" The want of stable *peace*, of which so many complain, may arise from imperfect views of the Spirit's love. True, our peace comes from the one work of the Substitute upon the Cross, from the blood of the one Sacrifice, from the sin-bearing of Him who has made peace by the blood of the Cross. But it is the Holy Spirit who glorifies Christ to us, and takes the scales from our eyes. If, then, we doubt His love, can we expect Him to reveal the Son in our hearts? Are we not thrusting Him away, and hindering that view of the peace-making which He alone can give? . . . Perhaps the want of *faith*, which we often mourn over, may arise from our not realizing the Spirit's love. ' Faith' (no doubt) ' cometh by hearing, and hearing by the word of God ;' yet it is the Holy Spirit who shines upon the word ; it is He who gives the seeing eye and the hearing ear. Under the pressure of unbelief have we fled to Him, and appealed to His love? ' Lord, I believe ; help Thou mine unbelief,' may be as aptly a cry to the Spirit as to the Son of God. He helpeth our infirmities ; and in the infirmity of our faith He will most assuredly succour us. It is through Him that we become strong in faith ; and He *loves* to impart the needed strength. He giveth to all men liberally, and upbraideth not. Yet in our dealings with Him regarding faith let us remember that He does not operate in some mystical or miraculous way, as if imparting to us a new faculty called faith ; but by taking of the things of Christ and showing them to us ; so touching our faculties by His mighty yet invisible hand, that, ere we are aware, these disordered souls of ours begin to work aright, and these dull eyes of ours begin to see what was all along before them, but what they had never perceived, 'the excellency of the knowledge of Christ Jesus our Lord'" (pp. 23-5).

So it is the "loving Spirit" who, having convinced us, testifies of Christ, and glorifies Christ, with the heavenly skill and power of a love as tender, as gentle, as it is divine. He brings the soul down into self-knowledge, into a *Know Thyself* of the true sort, and then He brings it up into the glorious counterpart, into the knowledge not of a "better self" but of Jesus Christ, in all the fulness of what He is. And He loves to do it. It is not only His eternally appointed, but surely also His eternally beloved work.

As we pass on let me call attention to Dr
Bonar's statements quoted just above regarding
the Spirit's gift of faith to us, and His mode of
giving.   My readers well know that it has been
a grave question whether the Spirit, whether
God, does " give " faith ; whether rather faith
is not just that which we have to contribute *of
our own store* to the work of conversion.   I am
indeed aware of the mysteries which connect
themselves with that question.   But I am quite
sure that Scripture does nevertheless teach us
that a living and saving faith is as truly a gift
Acts v. 31.   of God as is, for instance, "repentance."   I find this stated in Eph. ii. 8 ; a passage
where, if the context is attended to, the stress
of the argument is all in favour of explaining the
words "*and that* not of yourselves, it is the gift
of God," to mean that the matter just before
mentioned, namely the presence of faith in the
saved, is the gift of God.   I read the same
truth in the phraseology of Phil. i. 29, where
alike the power to believe and the call to suffer
are seen as "the gift" given to the saints.
And I see it very clearly, in a yet deeper
and more suggestive connexion, in 2 Cor. iv.

13, where the Apostle speaks of himself and his fellow-workers as "having the same spirit of faith" with the Old Testament saints. I believe the word "spirit" there to refer to the blessed Personal Spirit[1]; but that point is not necessary to the present purpose. What anywise the passage intimates is that faith is not of nature, but of grace. It is from above, not from the resources of human nature; it is the special and supernatural gift of God. I know the mystery involved, and indeed I feel it; but I entrust it to Him who, unlike me, knows the whole eternal case, and will one day gloriously justify those ways of grace which He calls us now to trust. And so I hold, and I am sure it is good to hold, that, where a man believes to life eternal, it will be made plain hereafter, if not now, that every link in the chain, not every link except one, was "mercy from first to last," and very special mercy too.

But then on the other hand[2] this view of the gift of faith, as Dr Bonar well puts it, does not

---

[1] See above, p. 9.
[2] How often, in pondering the things of God, we need to say "*on the other hand*"!

for a moment lead us to think of faith as of an alien or exotic something inserted, like a life-germ from another planet, into our nature. "Faith is trust," say what the Council of Trent[1] may. Our Lord's use of the word πίστις in the Gospels proves this. Faith is trust, reliance, personal confidence. And personal confidence, self-entrustment to another, is in itself a perfectly *natural* exercise of the human soul. What then is *super*natural, what is divine gift, about it in this great instance of saving faith? Why, surely, just that which can be illustrated from the experiences of human life, whenever anything "gives me confidence" in another. In such a case, the fact of my need being presupposed, and the fact of my con-sciousness of my need—the fact, for instance, of my knowing myself to be very ill—what "gives me confidence" in such or such a physician? The convincing manifestation to

---

[1] In the *Canons and Decrees of the Council of Trent,* c. ix. of Session vi. is devoted to the "refutation" of the *inanis hæretico-rum fiducia;* and Canon xii. of the Session anathematizes those who say *fidem justificantem nihil aliud esse quam fiduciam divinæ misericordiæ, peccata remittentis propter Christum.*

me of his personal trustworthiness.   Suppose
me fully conscious of my urgent need of a
physician, with a consciousness so strong that
ipso facto I am willing to use a physician, and
suppose the trustworthiness of that particular
man manifested to me by good proofs ; there
is thus and then "given" to me the gift of
faith in him.

Transfer this to the case of (not anyone
but) the awakened sinner.   The Spirit has
convinced him of his need—deep, wide, and
urgent—of salvation.   The Spirit now " takes
of the things of Christ, and shows   John xvi. 14.
them to " the soul thus prepared to behold
them to purpose.   The Lord and Saviour, in
His fitness, His adequacy, His unspeakable
trustworthiness, stands before it.   The need,
divinely shown, is met by the response and
the supply, divine and shown divinely ; and
the man lays his hand, sets his foot, upon the
Rock, because it is wanted and because it is
there.   He entrusts himself to his manifested
Saviour, and is His.   He believes, and it is
with a faith that is the gift of God.

It is important, if I understand the case at

all, to remember clearly in this whole matter
what in it is natural and what is supernatural.
The natural element is the action of a human
soul, conscious of exceeding need, accepting
the perfect provision for that need, seen to be
such. And from this point of view it is the
preacher's, and the private friend's, blessed
privilege and duty to point the awakened person
as directly, simply, and practically as possible
to the facts of the Lord Jesus Christ's Person,
work, willingness, love. No considerations of
the supernatural ought for a moment to disturb
that action, any more than if we were concerned
in recommending a tried physician to a friend
in illness. Only to-day it has been my duty
and my blessing to try to deal thus with a
wearied and burthened mind and soul ; and my
steady aim was, secretly indeed to invoke the
Spirit's grace, but also to point out in the
simplest and most practical terms the " reason
1 Pet. iii. 15. of the hope that is in us; " the central
certainty of the Resurrection of the buried Lord
of Calvary, and the light (amidst whatever
surrounding darkness) which that one precious
fact sheds upon all He did, and said, and is.

And with the effort to state the "reason of the hope" it was inevitable also to bear personal witness to the experienced reality of its power, the experienced mercy and love of this Risen Saviour, and thus to bring in the forces, so far as possible, of the sympathy of soul with soul. All this was, from one point of view, a natural proceeding; as natural as if I had been asserting and justifying my recommendation, on grounds of common reason and experience, of some medical or legal adviser of whose aid my friend stood in need. But all the while I knew full well that "God must give the   1 Cor. iii. 6. increase," God the Holy Spirit. I had a bright hope that He would use my poor reasonings and witness in order to bring the soul of my friend (who is very little likely ever to read these words) to a saving view of Jesus Christ; or that anywise He would *somehow* cause the *reason* of the Gospel to present itself satisfactorily to his mind. But well I knew that there needed also, in order to that man's believing unto life eternal, a special dealing by the Holy Ghost with those materials of argument and witness. It was needful that He,

divine and personal, should speak in ways
in which I cannot, and no man can, to the
depths of that spirit about " this same Jesus ; "
John xv. 26 ;   should " testify of Him " and " glo-
xvi. 14.   rify Him," as no man can, to that
human consciousness.   He must in His own
way make the facts more than mere facts, the
witness more than just credible, the Lord
more than an assured certainty of the past,
or of the unseen present ; even the ineffably
attractive magnet, desire, repose, of this
burthened soul.   The mystery of the Fall is
a fact.   Man's spirit does not of itself " see
beauty in Him that it should desire Him,"
(though no act of inward seeing is more
2 Cor. iii. 17, 18. absolutely reasonable,) until " the
Spirit of the Lord " gives that " liberty "
which comes along with a new grace-given
intuition into " the glory of God in the face
2 Cor. iv. 6. of Jesus Christ."

Thus, naturally at once and supernaturally,
the blessed Spirit "gives faith" in Jesus.   Naturally, by providing that the facts about Him,
and His work, and His love, shall come in
some genuine measure before the mental eyes.

Supernaturally, by bringing the soul, fallen from that original righteousness in which it was in sympathy and harmony with God, back into sympathy with the blessed facts. And this He does in part through His work of conviction of sin, and in part through shedding upon "the truth as it is in Jesus," in ways Eph. iv. 21. wholly of His own, a light of glory and beauty, or however of *reality*, which "eye 1 Cor. ii. 9, 10. hath not seen," but which "God revealeth by His Spirit." And so the soul sees, and the man believes and comes, entrusting himself to the divinely manifested Christ, and "believing, hath life through His Name." John xx. 31.

It is most true that saving faith is not always so given as that the *order of the process* of its giving can be described just as above. There are conversions where the process is, in a certain sense, reversed. Such a conversion was that of Count Zinzendorf,[1] the second

---

[1] Since writing this passage I have examined Bishop Spangenberg's *Life of Zinzendorf* (English translation, 1838), which as the work of the Count's intimate Christian friend is the best authority on such a subject as this. And I do not find all the statements in my text quite borne out. The narrative runs thus, p. 15:—"From [Frankfort-on-the-Main] they proceeded to

founder of the " Moravian " Church, the *Unitas Fratum*, with its marvellous missionary enterprises. His new birth to righteousness and God was wrought, so the story runs, through the sight of a picture of the Crucifixion, bearing the

Düsseldorf, where the Count's attention was particularly attracted by the excellent *Ecce Homo* in the picture-gallery, under which was the following inscription : 'All this I have done for thee; what doest thou for Me ? ' He reflected that he would scarcely be able to answer this question, and besought his Saviour to force him into the fellowship of His sufferings, if he should ever be disinclined to it." He was just nineteen at the time ; and his own account of his earlier years makes it plain that he both was, and knew himself to be, a believer long before that time. "It was my happiness early to experience a heartfelt impression of the Saviour ; after this all my wishes and desires were directed towards the Bridegroom of my soul, that I might live unto Him who atoned for me" (p. 3). But something not wholly unlike the account given in the text is alluded to in another extract (p. 4) from his own words :—"I was told [as a child] concerning my Creator, that He became a man. . . . I felt happy in conversing with Him, and grateful for His having remembered me for good in His Incarnation, But I did not wholly understand the greatness and sufficiency of His meritorious sufferings, nor was my own wretchedness and inability sufficiently obvious to me. I did also what I could in order to be saved, *until one extraordinary day*, when I was so much affected by what my Creator had suffered for me that I shed an abundance of tears, and attached and joined myself still more closely to Him."

On the whole I have preferred to leave the text as it stands, with this note. The experience which without quite adequate evidence is assigned in it to Zinzendorf is however an experience realized in many instances.

inscription, " *This have I done for thee ; what
hast thou done for Me ?* " He gazed, loved, and
rejoiced " with exceeding joy," turning from a
life of indecision at once, and without a pang,
to Christ. But do not think that the element of
conviction was absent in Zinzendorf's experience
as a whole. It came later, and with power.
And it was an element most necessary, as his
life-story shows, in order to save him from some
grave wanderings from sound faith in the matter
of Christian experience, and from a tendency
to drift away from a steady anchorage on the
atoning work of the Lamb of God.[1] And I

---

[1] I quote as follows from a French memoir (Bovet's, i., p. 224)
of his life :—" About this time I met with the work of Dippel, in
which the doctrine of Imputed Righteousness is attacked. Its
system seemed to aim at eliminating from the idea of God the
notion of His wrath ; and just so far as I sympathized with that
view I liked the system. I was then in the attitude of the natural
theologian ; and the 'good God' distressed me when His acts
seemed to lack a sequence of mathematical precision. I sought
to justify Him, at all costs, to men of reason. *But when I came
to think over my own conversion* I saw that in the death of Jesus
and in the word Ransom there lay a profound mystery—a mystery
before which Philosophy stops short, but as regards which
Revelation is immovably firm. This gave me a new intuition
into the doctrine of Salvation. I fonnd its blessing and benefit
first in the instance of my own heart, then in that of my brethren
and fellow-workers [in the *Unitas Fratrum*]. Since the year

am well assured that that after-gift of spiritual conviction tended in its turn only to deepen and develop for Zinzendorf the first gift of joy and love. The elements which we have dwelt upon as characteristic of conversion and its life were there, though the order of their arrival, if I may call it so, was abnormal. His faith in its sum total was the repose of the divinely awakened soul in the divinely manifested Saviour.

I appealed in my last chapter to my reader's own experience. May I do so again in this brighter and more blessed connexion ? In anything but an inquisitorial spirit, I do venture to say to you, has the Holy Spirit testified to you of Jesus Christ, glorified to you Jesus Christ, taking of His things and showing them unto you ? I do not ask, have you had this vivid crisis of consciousness, that almost vision of the unseen and eternal ? I am not one of those who speak lightly of such things, as if they were to be estimated off-hand

---

1734 the doctrine of the expiatory sacrifice of Jesus has been, and will for ever be, our treasure, our watchword, our all, our panacea against all evil, alike in doctrine and in practice."

as so many illusions, a discredit to sober
faith. Faith is magnificently sober as to its
grounds, and as to its nature. But when we
remember that what it clasps is JESUS CHRIST,
and what it receives is the life eternal and
the hope of glory, shall we think it necessarily
fanaticism if sometimes, and in some Christians,
" the sweet unveilings of His face " have been
such as even to agitate greatly the faculties of
the mortal tabernacle ?

> " My earthly by His heavenly overpower'd
> Sank down."

But I do not speak to you now of these
things, which certainly are not the *daily* " bread
of life." I only ask, has the Lord Jesus Christ
been so " revealed in you " that it is no forced
figure of speech to say that He has been
"glorified"? Has He been so shown to the
eyesight of the inner man as the Lamb of
Calvary that you not only hold (as it is so good
to hold) the clearest mental convictions about
Justification by Faith, as our Second and
Eleventh Articles put that great truth, but
that the Crucified, the Shedder of the justi-

fying blood, is *the adored and beloved* of your
awakened and confiding soul ?   Has He been
so shown within you as the Son of the Father,
the Only Begotten in the Father's bosom, that
you not only reject with fullest intellectual conviction the misbeliefs of a Sabellius, an Arius,
or a Socinus, in their oldest or their most
modern phases, but that your spirit does indeed
Ps. ii. 12.   " kiss the Son " with the deepest
homage of worshipping love, responding in
sweet harmony to the Voice out of the
Matt. xvii. 5. bright cloud—" This is *My beloved*
Son " ?   Has He been so shown within you
as your sovereign Master that you not only
reasonably own His claims but find that a
complete submission to them is pure happiness, because it is so real a means to *feeling
the bond* which unites you for ever to Him ?
Has He been so shown within you as your life,
your power, your wealth of resource against the
devil, the world, and the flesh, and your en-
ablement for humble service to His will, that
you not only applaud a spiritual theory, and
take pleasure in its exposition, but " *take
pleasure in infirmities*, that the power of Christ

may rest upon you," and His beloved   2 Cor. xii. 9.
presence be felt as it hardly can be felt without
the cross?

   Is it thus with you? Is it not thus with you?
It is a divine reality, is it not? Calm and pure
in its holy essence, this glorification of Christ
yet moves and thrills with a "joy unspeakable
and full of glory." And it is the   1 Pet. i. 8.
Holy Spirit to whom immediately the thanks
for that joy are due. You, convinced and
believing soul, reaping these fruits of living
faith in the Son of God, are a subject of the
best-beloved work of the loving Spirit. His
breath has moved the cloud for you from the
face of Eternal Beauty, and has quickened you
into the consciousness of what it is. "HE hath
been thus effectual in this secret work of your
regeneration unto newness of life;" in this new
birth "unto a living hope."   1 Pet. i. 3.

   Love Him, adore Him, give thanks to Him.
And meanwhile seek and expect His abiding
and continuous work of loving grace. Look
up to the Father, in this as in so many other
spiritual connexions, with the prayer, sure to
be answered, "Take not Thy Holy Spirit from

me." Expect, and humbly receive, not only
Ps. li. 11. an ever deeper view of the sinfulness of sin, but also an ever deeper view of
the glory of Christ, seen in the secret places
of present communion with Him and obedience
to Him. The Spirit will unfold more to you,
Eph. iii. 8 and yet more, of " the unsearch-
able riches" and their applications. He will
Eph. iii. 16, 17, " strengthen you in the inner man,'
19. so that " Christ shall dwell in your
heart by faith " with a blessed development of
continuousness and power, and so that you
shall " know the love of Christ," with the joy
of an ever new discovery.

> " Come, Holy Spirit, come,
> Let Thy bright beams arise ;
> Dispel the darkness from our minds
> And open all our eyes.
>
> " Convince us of our sin,
> Then lead to Jesu's blood,
> And to our wondering view reveal
> The secret love of God.
>
> " Show us that loving Man
> That rules the courts of bliss,
> The Lord of Hosts, the mighty God,
> The Eternal Prince of Peace.

" 'Tis Thine to cleanse the heart,
  To sanctify the soul,
To pour fresh life in every part
  And new-create the whole.

" Dwell, therefore, in our hearts,
  Our minds from bondage free ;
Then we shall know, and praise, and love,
  The Father, Son, and Thee."

So, a hundred and thirty years ago, wrote Joseph Hart ; and the need, the promise, and the prayer are the same this day.

CHAPTER VII.

WE have considered now, in our view of
the revelation through St John of the
Holy Spirit's work, three main passages dealing with that work. We have seen the Spirit
as our Regenerator from spiritual death into
John iii. spiritual life, and as our Convincer,
John xvi. and as the Glorifier of Christ in
the souls of the convinced. In this study
we have looked from different points of view
upon His supremely important function and
action in bringing the individual into that
living Union with the Son of God of which
we treated in a previous chapter. That
union, as we there [1] remembered, is altogether
by the Holy Spirit, and is normally effected
by Him through the processes of repentance

---

[1] Page 39. See also below, p. 131.

and faith, under which the man lays hold of and receives Him who is our Life, and receives in Him all His blessed fulness, the "grace for grace" of a perpetual John i. 16. and ever-new supply of the peace and power which is in Christ.

We have thus as it were seen the soul safe arrived at its Union with the Lord; and now henceforth its life, the whole life of the man thus united, is to be a new life, a spiritual life, a perpetual reception out of Christ following upon that initial entrance into Him. How then is this life to be led? Is the man now to take his spiritual affairs into his own hands? Has the Spirit led him up to his Redeemer, and there left him? No, most certainly. True it is that the experiences of this new life are to be as personal, as conscious, as truly voluntary (let us not forget this), as those of the old. "No will is so fully equipped for work as the regenerate will." The whole Scripture overflows with illustrations and reminders of that fact. Nevertheless the new life, if the man is living it indeed, is to have in it from first to last this divine and glorious new factor,

the inworking presence of the blessed personal
Paraclete, who in a sense now new and special
is both to guard and animate the " first springs
of thought and will," and above all to keep
alive, by continuous application of Christ, the
life He gave by first application of Christ.
Thus, in the words of a hymn dear to many
a believing heart,

> " Every virtue we possess,
>   And every victory won,
>   And every thought of holiness,
>   · Are His alone."

Following now our proposed method of
Scripture study, I keep still to the Gospel
according to St John, reserving for after study
the forms of truth given through St Paul.
And to illustrate from St John the work of
the Spirit in the developing experience of the
regenerate believer, I go again to the same
Paschal Discourse of our beloved Lord which
we have approached in the two previous
chapters. We have found there His own
account of some initial steps in the Spirit's
saving work. We shall now find there, in the

words of the same Teacher, a delineation of some of the inmost characteristics of the true life of His true followers, such as it was already in a measure then, and such as it soon was to become in rich development under the developed in-working of the Spirit.

In this whole delineation we have to re-member that although the Holy Spirit is only occasionally mentioned He is everywhere im-plied. For the discourse on the whole mani-festly deals with the disciples' experience in view of the withdrawal of the bodily presence of Jesus Christ. And the promised equivalent, and more than equivalent, for that presence, was to be the developed presence of the Comforter. As therefore the whole previous walk and life of the disciples had been bound up with the presence and power of their dear visible Master, so now their whole walk and life was to be bound up, in a connexion as necessary, tender, and powerful as possible, with the presence in them of this His holy Representative; by whom already they had come to believe on the Name of the Son of God and to be, however little they understood

it as yet, united to Him in the eternal life.
We read then rightly all through the Discourse,
and all through the High Priestly Prayer at
its close, the underlying truth of the work of
the Spirit, effecting every blessed experience
in the whole new life of the disciple.

And here let me point out the rightness of
referring these promises of the Paschal Chamber
not to the Apostles only but to us, to every
member of the believing Church. There are,
I doubt not, words in the Discourse and the
Prayer which have a primary reference to the
Apostles, and to their past and present experience, and to their coming work as the
Spirit-taught, infallible, teachers of the Church.
But there are indications everywhere that the
Apostles then, as on many another occasion,
were viewed by the Lord Jesus *not only* as
guides and teachers of the Church, but as
" the Church by representation," if I may use
the phrase.[1] In the fourteenth chapter, for
example, we find our Lord continually passing
from words bearing a primary special reference

---

[1] I owe the remark to my friend the Rev. C. H. Waller.

to the Apostles to words completely inclusive in their terms. "He that believeth   ver. 12. on Me, the works that I do shall he do also;" "He that hath My com-   ver. 21. mandments and keepeth them . . . I will manifest Myself to him;" "If a man love Me . . . We will make Our abode   ver. 23. with him." And indeed all through the great passage, with hardly an exception, we feel that it is rather the *Christian* life and character than specially the *apostolic* that is in view; the same life and character which the First Epistle of St John depicts and explains without any reference at all to special ministerial functions assigned to any sharers in it. So without hesitation or reserve I read these precious words of the Lord Jesus, spoken on the eve of His death and glory, as on the one hand bearing throughout on the work of the Spirit, and on the other hand applicable throughout to the life, needs, privileges, and possibilities, of every true believer. With these principles in mind let us come to the study.

I read then first in this Discourse some divine revelations about the Oneness of the saints with

Christ, and with the Father, and so with one another. "At that day" (the day, surely, of

John xiv. 20. the promised coming of the Comforter), " ye shall know that I am in My Father, and ye in Me, and I in you ;" "That

John xvii. 21, 22, 23, 26. they all may be one ; as Thou, Father, art in Me, and I in Thee, that they also may be one in Us;" "And the glory which Thou gavest Me I have given them ; that they may be one, even as We are one ; I in them, and Thou in Me, that they may be made perfect in one;" "And I have declared unto them Thy name, and will declare it : that the love wherewith Thou hast loved Me may be in them, and I in them." Ponder the words, as if you had never read them before. I well remember an occasion when they were thus brought forcibly and anew to my mind. It was an anxious hour of public religious discussion on the nature of the divine life in the Christian. One deeply earnest speaker carried his statements to a length which in my view was, as it still is, at variance with the holy proportion of revealed truth ; leading through truth out of truth to a related error which lay beyond

it. But God sometimes overrules even a manifest exaggeration or distortion to call attention
to something which it distorts but which we,
perhaps, have neglected and ignored. So it
was with me then. The solemnity, the intense
significance, the pregnant emphasis, with which
my friend and opponent that day repeated the
words of John xiv. 20: "At that day ye shall
know that I am in the Father, and ye in Me,
and I in you," sank deep into one heart at least
of those present and asked it whether there did
not lie in those words treasures of grace as yet
unsuspected and unclaimed; and so there did.
May I again, as I have done more than once
before, turn to my reader and ask if perhaps it
is so now with him? And if so, may I in my
turn entreat him to listen to those divine words
in the silence of the soul, as to a revelation
of principles, and powers, and experiences, and
possibilities, which have not the remotest necessary connexion with fanaticism but which may
nevertheless *mean* an inner life far different
from a life of fitful and intermittent faith, love,
joy, peace, and power for witness-bearing
and light-bearing for Christ? The verses

9

cited above from the seventeenth chapter
have, I well know, a momentous bearing
on questions of Church Unity, and are a
standing caution of the utmost gravity and
tenderness against the spirit of schismatic
separation and antagonism in external Christian
life.   But while remembering this, and reminding my reader of it, I must yet more
earnestly point out that the inner and intense
meaning of the words has to do with regions
of truth, life, and experience compared with
which even the sacred and important truths
of exterior Church Unity are a lower region.
It has to do primarily with the vital, spiritual,
Heb. xii. 23. eternal union of " the Church of the
firstborn written in heaven " with their glorious
Head, union in a life which is altogether of God
in its root and fruit.   It has to do with " knowledge " and experiences to which " the world "
is an utter stranger, with insights into everlasting love and joy coming down from the
Father of Lights, and with a cohesion and co-
operation, a united work and witness, which
depend absolutely for their possibility and power
on the recognition and following out of *such* prin-

ciples of union. Blessed will it be for Church
and for World when these principles shall so
vastly prevail as to find expression naturally
and from within in a harmonious counterpart
of order; a far different thing from what is,
I cannot but think, an illusory prospect—the
attainment of such internal unity by a previous
exaction of exterior governmental uniformity.

But this is by the way. My point is now
to call attention to the wonderful depth and
height, and personally searching and alluring
power, of these words of the Lord about Oneness, and then to remind my reader that the
realization of those words lies in the work of
the Holy Spirit. It is as HE unites me, and
unites thee, to Christ, by His new-creating and
life-giving touch and drawing, that we enter
into this amazing oneness with the Son, and
the Father, and one another; a oneness spiritually organic, in which each personality, while
quite exempt from *invasion*, falls under the
power of a divine *cohesion* whose results in
spiritual harmony of life and action will develop
for ever. " These things worketh that one and
the selfsame Spirit," blessed be His Name.

Along with this revelation of spiritual and Spirit-wrought oneness between the believer and the Lord, and between believers in the Lord, I gather up from this same Discourse many another precious kindred word. There is that great promise, " Because I live, ye shall _{John xiv. 19.} live also." It is a promise not merely of the Rescuer to the rescued, of the Saviour to the saved, of the Leader to the led, but of the Head to the limb, of the Vine to the branch. We rest on that promise, we _{Heb. xii. 2.} humbly believe it. " Looking off [1] unto Jesus," (very definitely and very necessarily "*off* unto " Him,) we appropriate it, and take it for granted, and act on it amidst the realities of life. " When thronging duties press," when by the providence of God we have to meet men, to walk up and down in the world of the present day, we yet fall back internally on the truth that "he that hath the _{I John v. 12.} Son hath life." The basis of our true being, the spring-head of our true life-pulse, is in Him. Even so ; and therefore, while He

---

[1] Ἀφορῶντες.

liveth, and because He liveth, we "shall not die but live." And this too " spake He of the Spirit." The Worker of this our abiding life is "the Lord, the Life-Giver," the Giver to us in inward reality of the Son who is our Life.[1] And shall we not bless His Name?

Closely in the same connexion I read here of blessed articulate experiences and realizations of this union and life. I read of "union turned into communion." I listen to the Son of God speaking not only to John and to Peter, but to me, that Paschal evening; and I hear Him say, "I will not leave you orphans; John xiv. 18, 19. I will come to you;" "The world seeth Me no more, but ye see Me;" "I will see you again, and your hearts shall re- John xvi. 21, 22, joice;" "I will manifest Myself to 23. him;" "My Father will love him, and We will come unto him, and make Our abode with him." I read these promises, coming direct from the lips of our Lord and Life, and I remember along with them those other words which He spoke out of His glorified life through

---

[1] See above, p. 39.

this same John : " To him that overcometh
Rev. ii. 17. I will give to eat of the hidden
manna ; " " I will come in to him, and will
Rev. iii. 20. sup with him, and he with Me."
And we bless Him for even the least realization of what they mean. And we remember
that it is the Holy Spirit who brings about
these realizations in us, who gives us to
know in any measure what is meant by
the indwelling and overshadowing of Jesus
Christ. And as we possess and enjoy this
wonderful, this infinitely merciful gift of the
known presence of the Son of God, and of the
Father in Him, we thank and adore the personal and gracious Holy Spirit that it is thus
with the soul.

"Shall I ever forget the summer morning,
in 1886," writes one whom I know, " when on
the sunny slopes of a Yorkshire moor, on a
brief holiday, not long after that blessed time
of spiritual discovery and strengthening in the
knowledge of God, I experienced indeed a ' joy
unspeakable and full of glory ' in the sight of
our Lord and Life ? Walking out alone I fell
into prayer, prayer to be conformed in all things

to the will of Him who had redeemed me and drawn me to Himself. As I proceeded, while heart and mind were kept in the deepest peace, and not the slightest enthusiastic disturbance of judgment was to be suspected, it was yet as if a heaven was opened around me, and the joy of the Lord flowed in divine effusion over my being. The glory and beauty of my Saviour's Person, the indescribable reality of His presence both in me and around me, the absolute 'all-sufficiency' of His grace and power, the loveliness and attraction of His 'perfect will'—all shone upon me with a brightness of which the August sunshine seemed but a type and a shadow. 'The Lord is my portion,' said the inmost spirit in that holy hour. In a sense, the glory passed away, as to special excitation. But in a sense, in a yet deeper sense, it abode, diffused among the experiences of life, and proving its 'sober certainty of waking bliss' by its power amidst these experiences, to calm, and purify, and lift above the selfishness of the old life." And "all this worked that one and the selfsame Spirit." It is by Him John xvii. 3. that we "know the only true God, and Jesus

Christ whom He hath sent," with that knowledge which is no mere result of information
and inference mentally collected. It is "eternal
life." Shall we not bless the Spirit's Name
that thus we know?

And so I may go on through the Paschal
John xv. 1-8. Discourse. I may take the Lord's
words about the True Vine, and the branches
which are in Him, and which abide or remain
in Him, and by virtue of their conjunction and
abiding bring forth fruit ; and under this whole
paragraph I .may read the presence and work
of the uniting and life-giving Holy Spirit. To
deviate for a moment to St Paul, and to a
Gal. v. 22.   passage with which we shall deal
more fully later,[1] we recollect that the sweet
fruit of holiness in the disciple's life is "the
fruit *of the Spirit.*" He it is who so works
in the man that, having "come to Christ"
John i. 12 ;   and "received Him," he also abides
vi. 37.   in Him as the days and years go
Deut. xxx. 19. on. The man freely and truly
"chooses life," welcomes and cherishes his

---

[1] See ch. x.

Lord's precious indwelling presence and power ;
but that he freely does so is of the gift of the
Holy Ghost. Because of Him, present and
inworking, the man "abides in the John xiv. 27;
love " of his Lord, and in His xv. 9, 11, 15.
friendship, and in His peace, and responds
with full joy to His joy. John xvi. 33.

And again, how much we have here about
the work and life of *prayer*! " Whatsoever
ye shall ask in My name that will John xiv. 13, 14;
I do;" " If ye shall ask anything xv. 16; xvi. 24.
in My name, I will do it;" " Ask, and ye
shall receive, that your joy may be full;" " I
have ordained you, that ye should go and
bring forth fruit, and that your fruit should
remain ; that whatsoever ye shall ask of the
Father in My name, He may give it you."
In those last words we have surely an indication of the deep, vital connexion between
true prayer and true fruit-bearing ; such that
the two things are as it were convertible terms.
It is as if He said, "I have ordained you to
produce real and lasting spiritual effects for
Me ; *in other words*, I have ordained you to
be, in Me, prevailing petitioners with My

Father that you may be bearers of such fruit." The "things asked of the Father in Christ's name" are that the disciple may be a vessel meet for the Master's use, a branch pregnant with holy fruit ; and there is therefore a deep and living correspondence between the bearing and the asking. Now here again is the opera- tion of the Spirit, "the Spirit of grace and Zech. xii. 10. of supplications." The prayer here meant is no mere devout performance of duty, the due utterance of an expression of reverence and dependence ; it is "prayer in Jude 20. the Holy Ghost," who "maketh in- Rom. viii. 26, 27. tercession for us . . . *according to (the will of) God."* It is the prayer of a heart filled with Him, and therefore filled with the humble but intense desire that His will may be done, and in particular that His implement may be used for His glory. Results of life, word, and work in answer to such prayer are "fruit that remaineth." And indeed it is "fruit of the Spirit."

I write[1] close to the tenth anniversary of the

---

[1] June, 1889.

blessed death of that truly sanctified servant of God, the late Miss Frances Havergal. Her life and work has just now been much in my mind, with its rich lesson and holy example. Speaking not for myself only but assuredly for a multitude of other readers, I may truly say that I never read her words of witness for our Lord without a sense of peculiar spiritual weight, influence, and holy persuasion, coming from those words to my heart. In a very marked manner her fruit seems to me to "remain;" the personal warmth and emphasis of her testimony "remains," as if the page had a living voice. And for my part I attribute this to the fact that while that devoted Christian was kept by the Spirit of God remarkably loyal to the foundation truths of the ancient and only Gospel of grace she was by the same Spirit led to, and kept in, an attitude of unreserved self-consecration to the holy Master's work and will which characterized her every effort, literary or otherwise, in His service. By the Spirit she asked to be fruitful, and by the Spirit she bore fruit indeed, "fruit that remaineth," and shall remain. In our measure. as we too are "vessels of the

Lord," let it be likewise with us, by the same secret.

Is it not somewhere in this direction that the humble Christian may look for God's fulfilment, in His own way, of that mysterious promise, John xiv. 12. " Greater works than these shall he do " ? Very possibly these words bear in their ultimate meaning not so much on the personal work of the individual Christian as on that of the Christian *as a member of* the Body and Bride of Christ ; as if to say, " He shall have .a real, living, full share in that wonderful work of ingathering and upbuilding Acts i. 1. which I his Master did but ' begin,' leaving it to My Bride to do more in *that* See Col. i. 24. *kind* than I had done." But such a view of the passage can only be true if it leaves clear the fact that wonderful possibilities of fruitful service are open, in the life of the Spirit, to the individual disciple who by the Spirit really lives and walks as a servant and implement of Christ.

John xiv. 26; xvi. 13; xvii. 7. Another class of passages in this divine Discourse bears explicitly upon the *teaching* work of the Holy Spirit

Here, I willingly and reverently own, we have a plain primary reference to the special knowledge and authoritative, infallible teaching of the inspired Apostles. But I do not think the words can be wholly limited to them. An instructive parallel is 1 John ii. 20, 27, where an inspired Apostle is addressing all the "little children" of his flock, and reminding them of their heavenly "unction," and of its mysterious power to give supernatural knowledge. And I gather from that passage that the true disciple is promised, not apostolic infallibility, but a more than natural instinct, in the use of divine revelation, to discern between essential error and essential truth in the things of salvation; a divinely given *feeling*, if I may put it so, for the sound word and against the illusory, counterfeiting substitute for it; and that this is the gift, the presence, the light, of the Holy Spirit in the soul regenerated by Him. Like many other great promises it needs to be read side by side with complementary and cautionary truths; but it is there, it is a reality, it is never to be forgotten, it is to be welcomed

and used.   And the Holy Worker is to be
blessed and thanked.

In closing I point to those precious words
of the High Priestly Prayer which speak of
the "keeping" and the "sanctifying" of the
disciples by the Father, who has given them
John xvii. 11,   eternal life in the Son : "Holy
15, 17.   Father, keep in Thine own name
those whom Thou hast given Me, that they
may be one, as We are ;" "I pray not that
Thou shouldest take them out of the world,
but that Thou shouldest keep them from the
evil ;" "Sanctify them in Thy truth ; Thy
word is truth."   Need we elaborately explain
that here the Spirit's work is to be seen,
though His name is not named ?   How in
fact was this prayer of the Son answered
in the life and history of the Church of the
children of God ?   It was by the effusion
of the Spirit, by whom, in a sense and mode
so large and full that it was more than com-
pensation for the seen presence of the Son,
the true members and the true body were
"governed and sanctified" in the new, wonderful life of the Gospel.   By Him they possessed,

and possess, the Father and the Son. By
Him, the Spirit of faith, they were, and are,
"kept through faith unto salvation." 1 Pet. i. 5.
"Praying in Him," they "keep themselves
in the love of God." Of the Jude 20, 21.
Father, through the Son, by the Spirit, comes
all keeping power, all sanctifying, separating,
consecrating grace. Let us adore the threefold Work; and now specially let us not forget, in our love and praise, the Third and
immediate blessed Worker.

So we leave the Upper Chamber. Or rather
so we close our enquiry into what was said
there by the Lord Jesus about the life which
is to be lived by us in the Spirit, only that
we may now and always "there continually
dwell." Amidst the stress and fulness of life
and duty, amidst the realities of trial and
temptation, there may we dwell indeed, in
internal recollection and experience, "sitting
at the table[1] with" our beloved Lord, John xii. 2.

---

[1] I need not point out in detail how large and rich, in the light
of the truths we have here considered, should be our fruition of
our life in Christ by the Spirit when we assemble at *the Lord's
Table*, the Table of the Paschal Chamber, at the Lord's most

leaning upon His sacred breast, and listening to His voice as He teaches us how to live that life of union, abiding, prayer, fruitfulness, spiritual insight, all under divine safe-keeping, which is laid up for those who by the 2 Cor. v. 17. Spirit are indeed "in Christ, a new creation."

---

loving command. Not that I limit for a moment the phrase in the text to Eucharistic occasions. Faith and love can turn *our social table* into "God's board" in a true sense; for certainly they can create a sanctuary in all the places and events of life.

CHAPTER VIII.

THE revelation through St John of the Person and Work of the Holy Spirit has now for some time occupied us. We go once more to the same great Apostle, before turning, as we shall then do, to the "beloved brother Paul."

In St John's Gospel there remain two passages in which the Holy Ghost is explicitly mentioned by the Lord Jesus, and whose messages to the believer, and to the believing Church, are of the weightiest import. In the First Epistle we have some few further precious contributions of truth on the Spirit's work. In the Revelation finally we have Him repeatedly presented, in His heavenly glory and in His work for men. Let us make this a chapter of fragments, taking up these successive passages each for brief remark and meditation.

10

(i.) John vii. 37-39.—Here stands the Saviour before us—" in the last day, that great day of the feast," the joyous Tabernacle Feast of Autumn, following with significant closeness on the Day of Atonement. The occasion must have been a scene impressive indeed in its externals. " After the priest had returned from Siloam with his golden pitcher, and for the last time poured its contents to the base of the altar; after the ' Hallel ' had been sung to the sound of the flute, the people responding and worshipping as the priests three times drew the threefold blasts from their silver trumpets—just when the interest of the people had been raised to its highest pitch, [it was then] that from amidst the mass of worshippers, who were waving towards the altar quite a forest of leafy branches as the last words of Psalm cxviii. were chanted—a voice was raised, which resounded through the Temple. . . . It was Jesus, who ' stood and cried, saying, If any man thirst, let him come unto Me, and drink.' Then by faith in Him should each one truly become like the Pool of Siloam, and from his inmost being ' rivers of living water flow.' . . . The effect was instantaneous. . . . Even the Temple guard . . . owned the spell of His words, and dared not to lay hands an Him. 'Never man spake like this man,' was the only account they could give of their unusual weakness."[1]

It was a voice mighty with the power at once of authority and promise. Above and through the mighty maze of symbolism it called the soul of man directly, without one intermediary film or interval, to "come to" HIM who spoke, to come with an absolute and therefore perfectly simple faith to HIM. And it promised, it guaranteed, with a self-evidencing majesty, that to all and several who should so come the very amplest blessing should result. The river of life eternal should so flow into them from Jesus Christ as to flow out through them to others. "As the Scripture had said,"—such Scriptures as Isai. xii. 2, 3 (observe the connexion of those verses) and lviii. 11,—"out of the belly" of each such believing man "should flow rivers of living water."

We are at once informed by the Evangelist

---

[1] Dr A. Edersheim, *The Temple and its Services*, p. 244.

of the meaning of the glorious imagery :—" This spake He *of the Spirit*, which they that believe on Him should receive." The reference was to the Holy Ghost, in His soon-coming development of presence and operation in the believing Church ; " for the Holy Ghost was not yet [given], because that Jesus was not yet glorified." Not, surely, that no rich and redundant blessing would have resulted then and there to each believer who took the Saviour at His word that hour ; but that in the great order of God's ways·such redundancy was not quite yet to be the rule, the open and manifest usage of grace. For must we not observe that, although the fullest allowance is to be made for large and bright exceptions, there was just this difference of *rule* between the spiritual conditions of the Old Dispensation and the New—that while the Old was a dispensation of conservation the New is a dispensation also, and in wonderful prominence, of diffusion and impartation through the New Israel and through the New Israelite ? To a degree altogether unprecedented this began to be at Pentecost. The Church, and the saint, were then so filled from above that

it was manifestly the purpose of the Lord that
not now and then only, and in exceptional cases
only, but all the true people of God always
should be open channels of blessing to men
around, conduits of life, by becoming living
vehicles for a living witness to the glory and
all-gracious power of Christ.   What Abraham,
and David, and Josiah, and Ezra, as regards
their personal life and its rule, were *not* altogether meant to be, the whole company of
believers, each and all, were altogether meant
to be now ; channels of effusion and diffusion
for the parched and weary world, in which they
were to live as men filled with the Spirit who
manifests and imparts the Lord.

Much might be said of course on questions in
detail which gather around this great truth and
principle.   We might turn aside to discuss the
question of the "miraculous gifts," and whether
they are at all in view here.   I think they are
not, for I think that here, as in the parallel
passage of the Well of Sychar, the   John iv. 14.
very tone and accent, so to speak, of the words
of Jesus Christ lead us straight to the needs of
the inmost human soul, and to the supply of

those needs. And those are needs which, be it said with reverence, would be poorly met indeed by even "unknown tongues" and "gifts of healing."[1] But I will not enter on any details of such a question here. We may be certain that, whatever else lies in these divine words, *this* lies in them—the assurance that the believer, the believer indeed, drawing the depth and fulness of the divine life from Christ by the Spirit, shall in his wholly subordinate way, yet in a way most real, be wonderfully used in the conveyance of that life around him. He shall not be an original fountain-head ; only One can be that. But he shall be a *living watercourse* ; a living secondary cause in others of living faith, and hope, and love, by the Holy Ghost. He shall not merely speak truth about Christ and the Spirit ; he shall speak it as living by it, as living it ; he shall Eph. iii. 20. speak by "the power that worketh in him" ; he shall touch his brother's conscience, and will, and love, with a contact whose power is not of him while yet it comes through him.

---

[1] See further below, p. 212.

If I may quote my own words written elsewhere,[1] the Lord "will use the man, or the
woman, who is really drinking the heavenly
water from the Rock, who is really filled for
life's needs with the supplies of life eternal, in
a mysterious way, and yet a way all the while
profoundly natural. Through that personality
the Spirit shall be pleased to work special
blessings, for He will have made it fit to be so
used. . . . It 'shall be a vessel unto   2 Tim. ii. 21.
honour, *sanctified and serviceable to the Master.*'
The believer in question may perhaps *know* that
he is thus privileged and employed, or he may
never know it at all. But that matters comparatively little." What matters is the promise
of the all-faithful Lord that we, even we, shall
somehow be channels for the lifegiving operation of the Eternal Spirit, on condition that we
"come unto Him," for ourselves, "and drink,"
and that we live "believing," live by faith in
the Son of God.

Blessed be He for such a promise, and for
such a condition. Blessed be the Spirit who

---

[1] *Thoughts on the Spiritual Life,* p. 147.

wills to flow forth, true to that promise, through the being of even us.

(ii.) John xx. 21-23.—We step here into a very different scene. The stir and festal triumph of the Tabernacle Day are hushed. It is the glorious calm of the evening of the first Easter, in that large Upper Room, so carefully barred and bolted, where the disciples with gladness saw the Lord. I need not recite at length His blessed words, the very first words addressed to them *as a company* by Him who now stood there amongst them in "the power _{Heb. vii. 16.} of an endless life." Enough to remember that they were words first of divine peace to themselves and then, immediately, words of mission, mission into the world, with a view to the "remitting" and "retaining" of sins. And this mission was accompanied by a marked and deeply significant action: "He breathed on them, and saith unto them, Receive ye the Holy Ghost."

Here again we might turn aside to more than one enquiry by the way; for example to the question whether the Risen Lord's action of breathing was the sacrament, so to speak, of an

immediate, or of a coming, gift of the Spirit;
whether He then and there conveyed to them
a special afflatus, or significantly assured them
of the great afflatus so soon to come.   But for
our present purpose this enquiry is not necessary.
In either case we gather unmistakably from
the words and action some great spiritual facts.
We see that the mission was one for which a
special gift of the Spirit's power and presence
was required.   And we see that that gift was
to be given in the very closest connexion with
the Person and Work of the Lord Jesus slain
and risen again.   The symbolic Breath came
from His holy lips.   As on the Pentecostal
day so now it was " HE who shed forth,"
whether it was in act or in prospect, the Spirit,
His Spirit, the Spirit of Christ, the Comforter
in His blessed power, One with Christ, glorify-
ing and imparting Christ.

As regards the terms of the mission I do not
speak at length.   Illustrated by the recorded
work of the Apostles and other first preachers
of the Gospel, it is surely plain what they do
not mean.   They do not mean that the divine
pardon of the soul is so put in charge of any

man, or any body of men, as that for one
moment that man, or that body, even if the
body were the whole Church, can intercept the
soul's direct appeal to the Lord and His direct
voice of peace to the soul ; or can provide a
substitute for either.   If this were the place,
it would be easy to show how the claims of
the Roman Catholic priesthood (and all really
kindred claims) to act as intermediaries in the
actual conveyance of divine remission are quite
without ground either in Scripture or in really
primeval antiquity after it ; and how the application of the words of this passage to the
work of the Christian presbyter comes up not
till comparatively late in Church history ; and
how even when the words were first so applied
the reference was understood to be to what we
may call the Church's pardon rather than the
Lord's, to the ministry of exclusion from and
re-admission to the ordinances and fellowship
of the Christian community. [1] But it may
be enough now to say that Scripture itself

---

[1] See *The History and Claims of the Confessional* (Longmans),
by the present Bishop (Reichel) of Meath. And the author's
Outlines of Christian Doctrine, p. 226.

abundantly witnesses to the Apostles' own unconsciousness of the possession of a really mediatorial power and position ; as for instance in the words of St Peter to Simon Magus at Samaria. And the practically one ^{Acts viii. 22.} alternative interpretation here is that the remission and retention are declaratory. The messengers here commissioned are to make known, for the world's need, how sin is forgiven in Christ, and how it is not forgiven.

And we surely gather that this work for the Lord is the work not of Apostles only, not of the sacred Ministry only, distinct and special as its functions are, but of the whole true Church of Christ. More persons were present in the Upper Room than the Apostles. Certainly the two friends from Emmaus were ^{Luke xxiv. 33.} there, and those two had found on their arrival "others with" the Eleven. And the Lord is at no pains to draw distinctions on this occasion, as He had been on others. No, He was empowering His whole true Church, there present by representation before Him, to be His delegate, His representative, in that part of His own mission from the Father which consisted in the unveiling to human hearts how sin is to be forgiven, how man is to enter into peace with God.[1]

So here is a passage in which every true child of God, every true member of Christ our Head, may read what is to be the essence of his own life-work for Him. It means no ecclesiastical anarchy, I am sure. The Lord is the

See 1 Cor. xiv. 33. God of order, not confusion. But it does mean that that is no true order which would debar the humblest Christian from his part, or her part, in this most blessed

Eph. iv. 12. "work of service," this earnest, Phil. ii. 16. loving, "holding out of the word of life." And on the other hand it solemnly, tenderly, reminds all such, as with the voice o Jesus Himself, that the inmost qualification for that work is not mere energy of character, or ease of utterance, or fancied fulness of knowledge, or even truth of view. It is the inbreathed and inbreathing presence of the Holy Spirit. If the message is to be not only true

---

[1] See Prof. Westcott's annotation on the passage. And see some remarks in an admirable book, the late Dr Hanna's *Forty Days after our Lord's Resurrection*, pp. 72-85.

but truly carried, truthfully handled, presented
as the solemn, blissful reality it is, the messenger, be he who he may, must be *spiritual*,
must possess, must be possessed by, the Spirit
of the Son of God.   The Holy Ghost must
have taught *him* indeed the realities of sin, and
of its remission.   The Holy Ghost must work
in and through him as in a vessel meet for the
Master's use.   If he bears the commission and
orders of the Church of God let him thank his
Master for the blessed privilege and advantage;
but let him not forget that the Church gave
him that gift *on the solemn understanding* that
he believed himself to be already, in a special
sense, dealt with for the purpose by the Holy
Ghost.   And let the lay worker for the Lord
equally remember that his title to be a witness-
bearer of the way of salvation is vitally connected, as between him and his Saviour, with
his being indeed spiritual, "worshipping by
the Spirit of God," "walking by the Phil. iii. 3.
Spirit," bringing forth the Spirit's Gal. v. 22, 25.
holy, humble "fruit."   So we come round
again, in essence, though under quite different
imagery, to the truth conveyed by John vii. 38.

(iii.) 1 John ii. 20, 27; iii. 24.—A very few
words will suffice on these two passages of the
precious First Epistle.   The former has been already treated incidentally,[1] and little more needs
saying here in this "chapter of fragments" than
to call the reader to observe the imagery of
"anointing" used by the Apostle.   The "little
child" in Christ is reminded by this that the
gift to him of the illuminating Spirit, who pours
through conscience, mind, and affections the
pure light of the eternal principles and truths of
grace, constitutes him in his new life a "king
and priest" to his Father, and, in a humble
but real sense, a "prophet" too ; a man who
has, under the guidance of the Word of God,
more than nature's insight into truth and error
concerning salvation.   The second passage,
with its truly heavenly context, will indeed
reward close and prayerful study as the believing
reader ponders the tender, gracious commandment (not commandments) to "believe on the
name of His Son, and to love one another;"
the love being the sure outcome of the faith,
just as far as the faith is true and full.   All that

---

[1] Page 141.

shall be said here is, of course, on the explicit reference to the blessed Spirit. What is its assertion? It is that the sure way to ascertain that God "abideth in us" is, to render the Greek literally, "out of the Spirit which He gave us." From that blessed Gift our proofs must be drawn. And how and where shall we find them? The immediate following context gives part of the answer; it is by finding our souls respond with a full Amen to the Scriptural revelation of the glory of the Incarnate Son and His precious work. And the whole New Testament suggests the rest of the answer; it is by finding our wills respond with a love and loyalty which only God can give to His own description of "the fruit of the Spirit," "His will, even our sanctification," His holy, humbling, chastening will.[1]

(iv.) A few words on the manifested glory and work of the Holy Spirit as seen in the Book of the Revelation shall close this chapter. The book abounds in mentions of Him. They range from i. 4—where beyond all reasonable

---

[1] See Dr R. S. Candlish, *The First Epistle of John* (Lecture xxviii.); a book of the highest spiritual value.

question the reverent Bible student will see Him, One but Sevenfold, in those Seven Spirits before the throne who are named *with and between* the Father and the Son as the Source of grace and peace—to xxii. 17, where the Spirit with the Bride, the blessed Life-Giver with and through the Body which He fills with the true Life, says "Come," to the thirsty soul of man asking for the living water which is given in the gift of Himself. I have touched already,[1] and perhaps sufficiently, on the beautiful phenomenon of Rev. ii., iii., the identification, or rather union, of the voice of Christ with the voice of the Spirit. It may be enough further to call attention to that one

Rev. v. 6; see glorious passage where the exalted
iii. 1.   Redeemer, recent from the wounds

of the Cross, is seen "having seven horns and seven eyes, which are the seven Spirits of God, sent forth into all the earth." The imagery, sublime in its boldness, carries manifestly with it some great truths concerning the relation of the Holy Spirit to the Lord

---

[1] Above, p. 10.

Jesus and to His presence with His Church below. It reminds us with peculiar and vivid force of the depth and closeness of the connexion of life and work between the Spirit and the Son. It shows us, "in the visions of God," how the Spirit is inherent in the Son, if I may dare to say so, inherent with an unspeakable union of being, and harmony of will, and order of working; and how He is sent forth by Him, radiates forth from Him. In particular it indicates that the glorified Christ, in all the exercises of His perfect Power (the "seven horns") and most real Presence (the "seven eyes") "in all the earth," in all His dealings with and for His people here below, has, for the divine Vehicle of that power and presence, the Holy Ghost in His sevenfold perfectness of gift and working. The effluent presence of the Lamb, if I may use the phrase, is made, is conveyed, for us on earth, for all the members "in all the earth," by the Holy Ghost. It is He who in perfectness of power "strengthens us in the inner man" Eph. iii. 16, 17. that Christ in perfectness of presence may "dwell in our hearts by faith." It is by

11

Him that we are "joined unto the Lord." It
_{1 Cor. vi. 17.} is He who makes the "one body,"
_{Eph. iv. 4.} by the union of each believer with
the Head, and so with all the members. The
force, the presence, the voice, of the Lord
Christ Jesus—all is by the Spirit; not by
physical, or quasi-physical, contact with the
glorified Body of the Redeemer, but by part
and lot in His Spirit.[1]

"Where that Spirit is," said the Dean of
Llandaff a few years ago in the Cambridge
University ·pulpit, "there is the Body of
Christ; and only there."

Come, then, blessed Spirit, evermore come,
and in all the sevenfold fulness of Thy infinitely
gracious operation bring us the members into
an ever deeper union, spiritual, heavenly, holy,
with Him who is our Head.

---

[1] I may refer in passing to a passage in Bp Jeremy Taylor's
treatise *Of the Real Presence* (Sect. vii., 8), where he examines
the process of divine benefit in the faithful recipient at the
Eucharist: "The benefit reaching to the body by the holy
Eucharist comes to it by the soul; . . . therefore by faith, not
by the mouth." The words have a special argumentative reference, but also touch the general subject of the mode of the
mystical Union.

CHAPTER IX.

WE approach the revelation of the blessed Comforter and His work given to us through St Paul. In the present chapter we shall attempt a sort of conspectus of the subject, and in the remaining chapters seek to take up in more detail some of the greater and more commanding truths thus given.

It is a large and wonderful field. The writings of St John, as we have seen, present us with a mass of treasure for our doctrine of the Spirit. On the great subject of His Personality in particular their witness is supreme in importance. But the Epistles of St Paul fairly overflow with the glorious theme of the Spirit and His work, and in respect of some of His great redeeming and sanctifying operations their witness is practically unique. Is not this remarkable, let me ask by the way, this fulness

of the doctrine of the Spirit *in St Paul*? We
are accustomed, and rightly, to regard St Paul
as the great commissioned teacher and vindi-
cator of that other region of vital truth—our
Acceptance, our Justification, for the Redeemer's
merits, by faith in His blood, by simplest acceptance of the divine imputed Righteousness.[1]
It is then all the more impressive to find that
to this same St Paul we must go for the fullest
scriptural account of "Christ in us" by the
Spirit as well as of "Christ for us" in His
merits. If the precious sentences, "Justified
Rom. iii. 24, 26. freely by His grace, through the redemption that is in Christ Jesus"; "That He
might be just and the justifier of him that believeth in Jesus," are deeply and distinctively
Pauline, so too are those others, "Your body
1 Cor. vi. 19. is the temple of the Holy Ghost
Rom. v. 5. which is in you"; "The love of
God is shed abroad in our hearts by the

---

[1] On that side of doctrine I may refer to Hooker's great *Discourse of Justification*, and to G. S. Faber's *Primitive Doctrine
of Justification*. I venture to add, as giving briefer or more
popular statements, my own *Outlines of Christian Doctrine*,
pp. 183, etc.; *Union with Christ*, pp. 65, etc.; and *The Lord our
Righteousness*, a tract.

Holy Ghost"; "Strengthened with might by His Spirit . . . that Christ may dwell Eph. iii. 16, 17. in your hearts by faith"; "Be ye Eph. v. 18. filled with the Spirit"; "Walk by Gal. v. 25. the Spirit"; "By the Spirit mortify the deeds of the body"; and so on, through Rom. viii. 13. a long chain of utterances living and glowing with the blessedness of our divine life, and peace, and strength, and "joy in Rom. xiv. 17. the Holy Ghost." In this double phenomenon of the writings of St Paul—this large and jealous vindication on the one hand of the way of our Acceptance through "the obe- dience of the One" and through it Rom. v. 19. alone, and yet this even more pervading and continuous assertion of our life and walk by the Spirit on the other hand—I read great and pregnant lessons. For one thing I learn that what God has so joined together man must not from either side put asunder, in faith, or teach- ing, or life. Perfectly distinct in conception, the two ranges of truth are indissolubly wedded together in purpose and in result. And for another thing I learn that in some all-important respects the one of these ranges of truth exists and is revealed for the sake of the other, and not the other for the sake of the one. Justification, Acceptance, Peace with God, Redemption from the Curse of the Law—these things are revealed (thanks be to God, they *are* revealed) not for themselves, so to speak, as if they were ends and goals in the way of grace, but for the sake of our living by the Spirit, and walking by the Spirit, and being the living temples of the Spirit, and thus being conformed to the image of the Son of the Father, and entering thus on a never-ending course of "serving in the newness Rom. vii. 6. of the Spirit." St Paul's writings, alike in their argument and in their proportions, are inspired reminders to us how to keep these things related in our own thought, and faith, and life. We are redeemed from the just sentence of the broken law " *in order that* we may receive the promise of the Spirit by faith ;" so it stands explicitly, and most memorably, in Gal. iii. 13, 14. Not for one moment, really, are we viewed as simply saved from present and future wrath as if that were an end in itself, the change of our hearts and lives coming in merely as evidence that we are secure. That change is, we may boldly say, the absolutely necessary *raison d'être* of the work of ransom and acceptance. We are accepted that we may be holy ; that we may live entirely to the Lord ; "that Christ may be magnified in   Phil. 1. 20. our body"; in other words that the blessed Spirit, now as it were liberated to flow upon us and to spring up within us, may have His way and will in all we are and all we shall be for ever.

Is it not so ? And shall not our faith, our witness, our teaching, take this apostolic line ? Shall we not stand fast, faster than ever, in the truth of the Justifying Righteousness received by faith alone, but so as always to enjoy and to commend the always related and always crowning truth of "the promise of the Spirit," received also by faith alone ? Happy the soul which, standing on the rock of the one truth, drinks the inexhaustible fountain of the other, day by day, and hour by hour. Happy the Church where that rock and that fountain alike "do follow them," in the work of witness in word and in life to the reality of God in Christ.

"So Christ shall be our daily food,
   Our daily drink His precious blood ;
   And thus the Spirit's calm excess
   Shall fill our souls with holiness." [1]

But it is time to come to some more detailed
view of what St Paul was guided to say of the
glory and work of the Holy Ghost, and of the
believer's dependence on Him and power in
Him.   Our view will not profess, however, to
be at all exhaustive ; the reader will find abundant gleanings left in the blessed field.

(i.) The witness of St Paul to the *Personality*
of the Spirit, though less full than that of the
Lord Jesus in St John, is unmistakable to the
submissive reader.   Nowhere indeed in St
Paul (in the Greek, though here and there in
e.g. Rom. viii. our Authorized Version) do we find
27; 1 Cor. xii.
11.   masculine pronouns, He, Him, His,
used of the Spirit.   But we find in St Paul

---

[1] Chandler, from St Ambrose : *Hymns of the Primitive Church,*
1837, p. 32.   The original Latin runs :—

   " Christusque nobis sit cibus,
      Potusque noster sit fides ;
      Læti bibamus sobriam
      Ebrietatem Spiritûs."—*Ibid.,* p. 163.

that the Spirit can be not only " quenched " but " grieved " ; that the Spirit " intercedeth for the saints with unutterable groanings," and that " He who searcheth the hearts " regards the Spirit, in that intercession, as the Bearer, the Subject, of a " mind," an intention, a characterizing thought. All this speaks of Personality. And we find the Spirit revealed, through St Paul, as the Lord of the "temple" of the Christian's body, and that in a context which is as remote as possible from associations of mere poetry or figure. A Person, and a divine Person, is presented to us here as dwelling in us.

1 Thess. v. 19 ; Eph. iv. 30.

Rom. viii. 26, 27; see ver. 6 in the Greek.

1 Cor. vi. 19.

(ii.) The unspeakably deep *Union of Being and Work between the Spirit and the Son* comes out clearly in St Paul. The Spirit is "the Spirit of Christ " ; and in the im- mediate context there we see the Two Blessed Persons so united that what in one breath is called the indwelling of the Spirit is called in the next the indwelling of Christ, and this again the indwelling of the Spirit.

Rom. viii. 9.

Rom. viii. 10.

Rom. viii. 11.

(iii.) When we come to the Pauline revelation of the *Process of the Work of Grace* we find that from first to last, from the new birth to the coming glory, the Holy Spirit is the immediate Agent, Life-giving, Life-sustaining. The true

Gal. iv. 29.

child of God is " born after the Spirit." He "lives *by* the Spirit."

Gal. v. 25 ; so render.

It is the Spirit who unites him to his Lord, his vital Head ; for " he that is joined " in the mystic bridal "to the Lord

1 Cor. vi. 17.

is one Spirit." It is the Spirit who in His own infinitely wise and effectual way makes known to him the reality and the sweetness of the eternal things so as he could not possibly know them by the powers

1 Cor. ii. 9-14.

of nature ; for "it is written, Eye hath not seen, nor ear heard, neither have entered into the heart of man, the things which God hath prepared for them that love Him ; but God hath revealed them unto us by His Spirit. . . . We have received . . . the Spirit which is of God, that we might know the things which are freely given to us (τὰ χαρισθέντα) of God. . . . But the natural man receiveth not the things of the Spirit of God ; for they are foolishness unto him, neither can he know them, because they are spiritually discerned." And this unveiling has to do, let us observe, not only with an eternal future but still more with a supernatural present. The main reference is to the present gifts of grace, the present and actual "riches of Christ," which are ours, now and here, in Him. "The things which eye hath not seen" are not only, as we read it in one of the loveliest and most pathetic of all English poems,[1] the things "beyond the clouds and beyond the tomb." They are the things which "*are, have been,* freely given to us of God." They are, in St Peter's magnificent words, "all things which 2 Pet. i. 3. pertain to life and godliness," and which now, as a fact, "His divine power *hath given us.*" They are a present fulness of divine acceptance, and a present fulness of divine spiritual riches;

"Our never-failing treasury, fill'd
With boundless stores of grace."

And so the Holy Spirit's work is to show us

---

[1] *The Better Land.*

what we *at this moment possess*, for our present
wonder, and joy, and use, and our present
glorification of the Giver.

This interior revealing work of the indwelling
Teacher, who is Creator too, is set forth in
detail in several passages of St Paul. Thus
we see Him, we hear Him, imparting to us a
supernatural insight into our blessed new childhood, new sonship, in the life and family of
grace, and a supernatural consciousness and
Rom. viii. 15.   assurance of it. "Ye have received the Spirit of adoption, whereby we
cry, Abba, Father"; "God hath sent the
Gal. iv. 6.   Spirit of His Son into your hearts,
crying Abba, Father"; "The Spirit itself
Rom. viii. 16, 17.   beareth witness with our spirit that
we are the children of God, and if children
then heirs." In some way of His own (let us
leave the details of the holy secret to Him) He
takes and teaches the believing sinner, and
shows him the strong, sweet, heavenly certainties
of the Word of God *as true for him*, so as not
the most exact nor the most profound exegesis
without Him could show them. Under His
mysterious touch of truth and love it becomes

strangely and gladly clear that the promises and welcomes of grace mean what they say; that " he that cometh " is " in no wise cast John vi. 37. out," and that this "not cast out" means a most glorious and wonderful "welcomed in;" a union, a filiation, an incorporation into the blessed family of God, in the divine Firstborn Brother, which implies beyond a doubt for the believing sinner all the adoptive privileges of sonship, and the full admission of the heavenborn child to the responsive intimacies of divine love.

The same view of the Spirit's work, though under less definite imagery, comes out in Rom. v. 5 : " The love of God hath been poured out " (so literally) " in our hearts by the Holy Ghost which is given unto us." This has been explained by some to mean that He has now imparted to us, in rich effusion, a divine *power or faculty of loving ;* has caused us to love with a love which is the love of God. I cannot but differ from such an exposition. With what it probably means at its heart, so to speak, I am entirely at accord. Fully assured I am that, while we can only love God with the same constitutional human faculty or moral organ, with

which we love man, still our union by the Spirit
with the blessed Head of regenerate manhood
has put such a new condition into that organ,
and connected it so with His love who is our
Life, that we may speak of our regenerate souls
as loving with His love ; "*in the heart of Jesus*
Phil. i. 8.   *Christ,*" as St Paul expresses it.
With inmost assent of mind and faith would I
echo those words of Miss Frances Havergal's :

> "Thy love, Thy joy, Thy peace,
>   Continuously impart
> · Unto my heart,
>   Fresh springs that never cease
>   But still increase." [1]

Only I would use them as remembering
always that this most blessed connexion and
infusion never invades our personality, nor
annuls our responsibility. [2]   But the context of

---

[1] *Hymns of Consecration and Faith*, No. 264.

[2] On this subject, our derivation of the whole secret of the
new life from our Head by the Spirit, see Marshall, *Gospel
Mystery of Sanctification.*   See particularly Direction iii., near
the beginning : " One great mystery is that the holy frame and
disposition whereby our souls are furnished and enabled for
immediate practice of the law must ' be obtained by receiving it
out of Christ's fulness,' as a thing already prepared and brought

Rom. v. goes clearly, as it seems to me, against our explaining "the love of God" here of our love to Him. It is "His love which <small>Rom. v. 8.</small> He commendeth toward us, in that, while we were yet sinners, Christ died for us"; a love altogether His, not in origin only but in expression and direction, while yet the manifestation of it to and in the heart of the justified believer has everything to do with his waking up to "love the Lord His God with all" that "heart." And it is this manifestation which the blessed Spirit effects; so we read here. Dwelling in the man He has regenerated, He so deals with the regenerate consciousness that the apprehension of mercy, the acceptance of acquittal, comes to be transfigured into an intuition into an

---

to an existence for us in Christ, and treasured up in Him; and that as we are justified by a righteousness wrought out in Christ and imputed to us, so we are sanctified by such a holy frame and qualifications as are first wrought out and completed in Christ for us, and then imparted to us; . . . so that we are not at all to work together with Christ in making or producing that holy frame in us, but only to take it to ourselves, and use it in our holy practice, as made ready to our hands." The whole context, and indeed the whole book, are the best vindication of this statement, which, in Marshall's sense of it, means to recommend anything rather than a life of spiritual indolence.

"everlasting love" as tender as it is almighty.
The man finds, he knows not how, outpoured
in his heart (ἐκκέχυται), that "rest of bliss," that
"sweet, pleasant, and unspeakable comfort,"[1]
which rises direct from the certainty not that he
loves but that he is thus wonderfully loved.

> " Loved with everlasting love,
>   Led by grace that love to know—
> Spirit, breathing from above,
>   Thou hast taught me it is so ! "[2]

We have here then a work of the Spirit of
Love, *supremely characteristic.* We shall see
the presentation of it in yet more developed,
vivid, and as it were concrete forms when we
come in a later chapter to study St Paul's
Eph. iii. 17. later written words about the
dwelling of Christ in the heart by faith. And
we find it, as we have already noticed, re-
appearing in this same Roman Epistle, where
Rom. viii. 16. " the Spirit itself beareth witness
with our Spirit that we are the children of
God." Observe the phraseology there. The

---

[1] Art. XVII.

[2] See the whole noble hymn (by the late Rev. Wade Robinson),
in *Hymns of Consecration and Faith,* No. 260.

Spirit appears as witnessing not to, but with, our spirit; a statement of the precious facts which gives us a view of them not so clearly given in ch. v. 5; for here, in viii. 16, we have "our spirit" brought in as a concurrent witness. On the Holy Spirit's part the "witness" is, "Doubtless thou art His child;" on our spirit's part the "witness" is, "Doubtless Thou art my Father," seen, welcomed, chosen, loved as such by even me. And the two distinct lines of witness meet in one strong, happy, humble certainty.

The man thus dealt with by the Holy One is seen, in St Paul, as the subject of His presence and power in many a sacred detail. In his human spirit he has so received the Spirit that he is said, wonderful as the phrase is, to have "the mind ($\phi\rho\acute{o}\nu\eta\mu\alpha$) of the Spirit," His moral characteristics. Our version of Rom. viii. 6, "To be *spiritually-minded* is life and peace," is inadequate while true. It fails to give, as the literal version does, the truth of the unspeakable connexion in the life of grace between the Spirit and the spiritual man; the glorious mystery of the Vital Union as it regards the Spirit's indwelling presence and power. Reading literally, " *The mind of the Spirit* is life and peace" (see ver. 27), we see the believer, mortal, sinful, the ceaselessly needy recipient of " mercy from first to last," yet so wonderfully visited and inhabited by his Regenerator, his Sanctifier, that along the lines of his own real will, understanding, and affections, there runs the power of the personal Presence, yea, of the personal Character, of the Lord the Life-Giver. The more the man humbly, and in watchfulness and prayer, but with entire willingness and simplicity, " yields Rom. vi. 13. himself unto God" thus present, the more shall he, intact in personality, have carried out in him the workings of that " mind." And what will the result be ? No sensationalism, no fanaticism. A great conquest and captivity will be one side of the 2 Cor. x. 5. result ; " every thought brought into captivity unto the obedience of Christ." A holy prayerfulness, deep and yearning, will Rom. viii. 26; be another side of the result. A see Eph. vi. 18, and Jude 20. loving, joyful, peaceful, trustworthy, meek, self-controlled walk in human life and

intercourse, will be another. A tendency to-
wards all such union with other chil- <small>Gal. v. 22, 23.</small>
dren of God as is obstructed by the <small>1 Cor. xii. 4.</small>
<small>Eph. ii. 18,</small>
life and spirit of self, will be another. <small>iv. 3, 4.</small>
<small>Phil. i. 27,</small>
A joy and delight in adoration, and <small>ii. 1.</small>
generally in being at the will and service of
the adored Lord, will be another. <small>Phil. iii. 3.</small>
A deepening consciousness of the truth and
conquering power of the Word of God, as the
sword in the spiritual combat, will <small>Eph. vi. 17.</small>
be another. A growing gladness in the ex-
perience of a meek and lowly but most real
sacrifice and surrender in all things to God,
will be another; as the believer realizes his
union, by the Spirit, with Him who "by
means of the Eternal Spirit offered Himself
without spot to God." A quiet <small>Heb. ix. 14.</small>
readiness, as one aspect of the same blessed
fact, to be "led by the Spirit," <small>Rom. viii. 14.</small>
will be another; and that leading will always
be *out* of the way and will of self *into* that
of God; out of the ambitions and interests
of self into a daily aim and inmost choice
and longing that "Christ may be <small>Phil. i. 20.</small>
magnified in my body," that I may "shew

forth the praises of Him who hath called me
<small>1 Pet. ii. 9.</small> out of darkness into His marvellous
light," that I may be, for the help of all
<small>2 Tim. ii. 21.</small> around me, "a vessel meet for the
Master's use," an implement ready to His
hand. And another side of the result of
having "the mind of the Spirit" will be a
larger insight into what is meant by a life of
faith, a life of unreserved reliance on the promises and will of God, a reliance ever more
childlike in its simplicity and ever more ma-
ture, and strong, and prevailing in its results.
For the faith by which Christ dwells in the
heart is but the effect in my soul and will of
<small>Eph. iii. 16, 17.</small> the blessed Spirit's "strengthening."
<small>2 Cor. iv. 13.</small> He is "the Spirit *of faith*." And
on the other hand it is "by faith," by the
simplest faith, that we "receive the promise
<small>Gal. iii. 14.</small> of the Spirit," as regards His
developed inworking and empowering.

And if we take that aspect of the regenerate
life which has specially to do with "victory
and triumph against the devil, the world, and
the flesh," the threefold ever-present enemy,
how great are the assurances given us in the

writings of St Paul, as regards the power
and working of the Holy Spirit! All Bible
readers are familiar with the antitheses, so
especially Pauline, between "the flesh" and
"the Spirit." But not all are familiar with the
fact, which surely comes out under any careful
enquiry, that by the Spirit, in such connexions,
the Apostle habitually means not a "better
self" or "nobler powers" of even regenerate
man, but the indwelling Paraclete Himself.
So that the man who "sows to   Gal. vi. 8.
the Spirit" means the man who casts the
seed so to speak of all life's experiences upon
that divine soil ; in other words, commits it to
the Holy Ghost within him to deal victoriously
with temptation and to put forth as the result the fruit of holiness. And the man who
in the realities of our life in the body, that
body which is practically our one immediate
vehicle of contact in all things with the world
around, "mortifies the machinations   Rom. viii. 13.
($\pi\rho\acute{a}\xi\epsilon\iota\varsigma$) of the body," does it, if he does it
indeed, "by the Spirit." He brings to bear
upon the whole range of motion and solicita-
tion to evil, incident to him as a dweller in

"this tabernacle," the glorious fact that "he is joined unto the Lord, one Spirit;" that His "body is the temple of the Holy Ghost, which he hath of God, and that he is not his own." He recalls Gal. v. 16, 17: "Walk by the Spirit, and ye shall not fulfil the lust of the flesh; for the flesh lusteth (ἐπιθυμεῖ) against the Spirit, and the Spirit against the flesh; and these are contrary the one to the other; so that ye cannot do the things that ye would." Is not that passage too often read as if ver. 17 had nothing to tell us but (what it assuredly *does* tell us) that the "infection of nature doth remain, yea, in them that are regenerated,"[1] and that to the last? True; it is a truth of constant merciful humiliation and caution. But what is the main purpose of the Apostle in this passage? Is it not emphatically to press the bright side of the antithesis, the side of peace, and victory, and liberty, and power? Its message, in the context, is altogether one of encouragement. It is written, like the treasures of truth in 1 John i.,

1 Cor. vi. 17, 19.

---

[1] Article IX.: *Manet etiam in renatis hæc naturæ depravatio,* etc.

"in order that we may not sin." St Paul is
intent on showing the believer how, 1 John ii. 1.
although "the flesh" is always present, carrying
with it always the ingredients, so to speak, of
the experience analysed in detail in Rom. vii.
7-24, there yet is something else always present
also, and present in force. It is " the Holy
Ghost given unto us." It is the living and
personal Comforter, dwelling in our body, and
making present in us " the life of 2 Cor. iv. 10, 11.
Jesus." It is the Spirit "lusting against the
flesh "—a force, a tendency, a personal Power,
on the side of our deliverance and victory,
gloriously competent to overcome its antagonist, and to make us, the subjects of it, as we
yield to it and welcome it, mercifully " *unable
to do the things we would*" in the life of the
flesh, in the life of self.

So " there is liberty where the Spirit of
the Lord is " ; a blessed liberty, 2 Cor. iii. 17.
meek and lowly, but strong and thankful
too. We find an emancipation from " old
sins," and a wonderful precaution 2 Pet. i. 9.
and prophylactic against new ones, in the
secret of an indwelling strength, or rather

Strengthener, who is not ourselves yet is as
near to us as ourselves.   He is at the same
time our always enlightening Convincer, as He
unfolds to us the divine Holiness and our " exceeding need."   But also, blessed be God, we
shall find in Him, as we welcome Him, our
internal Liberator, present always, not sometimes only ; our "victory and triumph" in a
way which forebodes no exhaustion by its
own efforts, for it is the Almighty One working
in us.   We come very quickly, in the interior
conflict, to the edge of our own strength.   But
to rest upon the presence of "the Spirit lusting
against the flesh" is to repose upon a Power
which has no edge, and no bottom.   And
conscious weakness is that which reposes most
simply and most effectually upon it.

Let me close this brief general view with the
remark that no call is louder to the Church,
and to the Christian, of the present day than
that we hasten to discover (if we still have that
to do), and then always watchfully to use, our
"great strength" in the Spirit of God for
deliverance from "serving sin," that so we may
be filled with His "calm excess," and may

overflow for blessing in the world around. The call, for one and for another, may not be to a life of any extraordinary apparent sacrifice, or external exhaustion or hardship; though who may say that it shall not be so? But most assuredly, for all who would be on the Lord's side in these days of ours, it is a call to a life of just such "coming out and being separate" from the world externally (while yet we are ready every hour lovingly to serve that world for our Lord) as arises from a true separation from the life of self and of sinning internally. How shall it be? How shall we indeed be sanctified, sinners that we are, in order to this witness and service of word and work? There is only one way. It is "in 1 Cor. vi. 11. the name of the Lord Jesus, and by THE SPIRIT of our God."

CHAPTER X.

A GENERAL view of the revelation through St Paul of the Holy Spirit and His work lies now before us. We proceed in the chapters which remain to a more detailed study of some leading Pauline passages, in which the Spirit's blessed operation and its results stand out manifested with peculiar glory.

May our "meditation of Him," by His great Ps. civ. 34. grace, "be sweet." May thought and word be in some true sense His, and may the whole result be for Him.

I take up in the present chapter the great passage about the FRUIT of the Spirit, generated and produced in "the spiritual man." The Gal. v. 22, 23. words thus specially before us are part of a context, and indeed of an Epistle, full to overflow of the truth of the Holy Ghost. What we observed in the last chapter regarding the doctrine of St Paul in general is seen in the Galatian Epistle, and in this section of it, eminently.

The Epistle is an urgent protest against a false doctrine of Justification. It states with strong and jealous firmness and precision the truth of the finished work of the atoning Cross, and the absolute necessity and simplicity of the function of faith, faith only, in order to the sinner's entrance into the merits of the Crucified, into acceptance in Him who "bought us out from the curse, being made a curse   Gal. iii. 13. for us." It protests that a Gospel which leaves this out, which has not this for its message, is not a Gospel but a fatal perversion of the Gospel. But does the Epistle stand still there? Is Justification its whole message? No; it conveys quite as much a warning, a testimony, an affirmation, about the work and power of the Holy Ghost. The all-importance, for St Paul, of the truth of Justification resides after all in this, that for the justified, and for them only, lies open the life, and walk, and victory, and fruit-bearing, which is by the Holy Ghost alone. As guilty sinners they take refuge by faith in

Jesus Christ "made a curse for them;" and then, and so, they become possessed of all that is laid up in that same Saviour risen and glorified, and who now by the same Spirit who led them to Him dwells in them.

So in this Epistle of Justification, as it draws to its wonderful close, we have more and more of the Holy Ghost. "Walk by the Spirit, and Gal. v. 16. ye shall not fulfil the lust of the flesh;" let us observe the definiteness and decision of that promise, my Christian brother and reader, and humbly claim it. Again, "The flesh lusteth against the Spirit, and" (we dwelt on this divine side of the matter in the last chapter) "the Spirit against the flesh." Again, "If ye be led by the Spirit, Gal. v. 17, 18. ye are not under the law;" not in collision with it, as it is the royal proclamation of your Father's will. Do you challenge His inspection as solely and only JUDGE? Ah, that would to the last involve a sternly judicial condemnation.[1] But do you lovingly, and with

---

[1] Observe the well-weighed words of Article XII.: "Good works, which are the fruits of faith, and follow after justification, cannot . . . endure the severity of God's JUDGMENT."

the heart of the child born again of the Spirit, look up to Him as FATHER, and, giving yourself to be led along the way of His will by His Spirit, say, "Oh how I" (not Ps. cxix. 97. challenge, but) "love Thy law," Thy will revealed? Then indeed, as regards your personal relation to that law, you are not "under it;" it is not "over you" as the judicial sword. Not only has your blessed Redeemer met it for you as you have violated it, and as you fall short of it; you also now, in a sense most humble, led by the Spirit, meet it with the sincerity of a loyal will, loving the Lawgiver "from the soul." Eph. vi. 6; so literally. Again, a few verses later, comes the significant precept, "If we live by the Spirit," if indeed we have by His power the new birth and life, "let us also *take step by step* (στοιχῶμεν) *by the Spirit.*" Let us consciously, with recollection, and *in detail*, apply our life-power, yield to our Life-Giver, in the daily path. Not only as to the large scope of existence but in the minutest things of this hour, in the small but strong temptations of ordinary intercourse, in the facile

commonplace occasions for loss of temper, loss
of humility, loss of purity, failure to love, to
serve, to remember that we are not our own,
let us "take step by step" by the Holy Ghost.
Can I too earnestly press that precept, with all
its speciality of phrase in the Greek, upon my
reader, upon myself? Again, a little further
_{Gal. vi. 1.}   on we have "the Spirit *of meek-
ness;"* the blessed Paraclete ready to guide
us "step by step" through one of the specially
rough and crooked places of common Christian
life. And a little lower again, in a passage
_{Gal. vi. 8.}   which we touched upon in the last
chapter,[1] we find the Christian entreated to
"sow to the Spirit," to cast, by faith, upon
the presence and power of the Holy Ghost
within him, as upon a divine soil, the seed
given by each trying incident of life. The
issue of such sowing shall be "life everlasting;" developments of the life of God within
him now, and eternal developments from each
such sowing hereafter, to His glory.

But I must not pursue too far, though it is all

---

[1] Page 181.

to the purpose, the context of our special passage, nor the general teaching of this Epistle on
the relations between acceptance in Christ and
life by the Holy Ghost.   We come now at once
to a view of the FRUIT OF THE SPIRIT.

Here first observe the light thrown by contrast on the word "fruit."   Just be- Gal. v. 19-21.
fore we have had recounted to us "the *works*
of the flesh."   The difference of the phrases
is significant.[1]   In the one the noun in question
is plural, in the other singular.   A weary course
of discords and internal collisions, a life in pieces
and out of joint, is thus contrasted with a life
whose growth is one harmonious development
from one rich central principle, germinating
and *fructifying* into a result of purity and
peace.[2]   Here is already a lesson for the
spiritual man.   As far as the Holy Spirit is in
possession of him, as far as he is being led
by the Spirit, and is yielding himself to the will

----

[1] See some excellent remarks on this point in the Rev. Hugh
Macmillan's *True Vine*, p. 142.

[2] I do not mean that the word "works" can *of itself* suggest
the meaning above given.   This would be obviously untenable.
But its position here, close to "fruit," and in antithesis to it,
suggests that meaning.

and mind (φρόνημα) of the Spirit, so far is his
Rom. viii. 6. life set free from the internal wear
and restlessness of "the works of the flesh,"
and drawn together into a peace and unity
which is possible only where what is made
for God rests in Him and lives for Him.

But this singular number, this " Fruit," not
" fruits," of the passage before us, has more
to say, besides this lesson of contrast. It reminds the Christian, as he reads over the blessed
list of elements in the heavenly Fruit, that
they are essentially parts of one thing, and not
isolated things, in the Lord's idea of the servant's life. They are not separable characters,
but a character. They are not put before the
man who "lives by the Spirit" in order that he
may pick and choose, and prefer to develop
some one or two of them, perhaps those which
he feels instinctively have most affinity with his
natural dispositions. They are in the divine
intention always inter-related, indivisible ; the
whole character of the Christian. We may
Matt. v. 3-12. compare the Beatitudes, which assuredly describe not various persons but one
person, the true disciple of Jesus Christ seen

from many points of view. And we may compare also that remarkable passage, 2 Peter i.
5-7, where, under widely different phraseology,
the believer, the man who has "obtained
precious faith," is entreated to "give all
diligence" to seek for a holy completeness and
harmony in the manifestation through him of
the life of God which is in him.

That passage, by the way, may caution us
against a disproportionate inference from the
precious imagery of "the fruit" in this. The
ideas suggested by fruit and fruitbearing are
not those of effort and care in the fruitbearing
branch ; effort and care are the cultivator's part.
But St Peter reminds us that the analogy
between the impersonal fruit-tree and the personal believer cannot be in all respects complete.
In the conscious and responsible man, as such,
there must always be place for " all diligence."
Such " diligence " does not create life, or
generate it, nor does it in a direct way develop the issues of life. But diligence is the
believer's duty in connexion with that development ; it means, if done in spirit and
in truth, the believer's " laying   1 Pet. ii. 1.

13

aside," in the Lord's name, every known thing that *hinders* the outgrowth and fulness of the fruit.

But when this is said, by way of balance and clearness, then without reserve we can throw our thankful attention upon the blessed suggestions and significance of the word "fruit." What does it tell us? It tells us, the branches of the true Vine, that in us, yet not of us, there is a mighty fructifying PRINCIPLE. It tells us that the holy characteristics, the holy character, here painted before us must not be worked up by weary efforts out of the materials of self, somewhat re-adjusted and assisting one another's weakness, if they could do so. The happy, pure phenomenon has a nobly adequate vital CAUSE behind it. It grows; it is not manufactured. It is not acquired from our surroundings, but produced amidst them. It is the result of a secret of LIFE; Life, that most wonderful of forces, while most silent; the force which in the natural world can, in the tender shoots of the young tree, lift the massive stone, and rend the joints of rock-like masonry; and which in the spiritual

world can make the weak strong, and do
silent miracles with what once seemed impos-
sibilities in character within and circumstances
without.

Let the anxious, the discouraged, Christian
ponder this word "fruit," recollecting this its
special significance. Let it remind him where
his "great strength" lies. It lies in *nothing*
that is properly and personally his. All that is
his, all such that is not sin, is capable indeed of
wonderful use by his "great strength." Gifts,
talents, faculties of mind, or body, or estate, be
they very large or very, very small, all are
precious, all are usable. But none, absolutely
none, is his true strength. That lies wholly in
a divinely given secret, principle, force, which
is in him but not of him, and whose power is
not for a moment to be measured by his weakness. "From it is his fruit found." See Hos. xiv. 8.
Let him be at rest about the adequacy of
that Cause to produce the effect of holiness.
Let him in humble faith "lay aside" all
known hindrance; and then in the same
humble faith, watching and praying, but not
struggling to force out the mighty Life, let

Rom vi. 13. him "yield himself unto God" for a divinely natural fruitfulness.

For this fruit is "the fruit of THE SPIRIT." Here is the all-important and all-welcome fact for us, in our present enquiry. This vital secret, force, principle, of which we have spoken —what is it ? No abstract truth, no ideal of duty, no awe-inspiring but never life-giving "*I ought.*" It is the Holy Ghost, the Personal and Loving Paraclete. It is the Lord, the Life-Giver, whose tender and mighty working has drawn me to Christ, and knit me into Him, and imparted Him to me ; blessed be His Name. Because of Him, by virtue of Him, thanks to Him, through Him in-dwelling, in-working, filling, welcomed in to have His way 1 Cor. vi. 19. in His temple, the fruit of holiness begins to be, to grow, to come forth, to take its gracious shape, to ripen into its sweetness for the service of God and Man. And so our way, our indirect way, to contribute to the blessed result is clear. It is to remove in His name the obstacles, but then to re-member with thankful and peaceful joy that the work of life-giving and fruit-producing is

His alone. *From this point of view*, my part is a blessed and wakeful Quietism[1]; a rest, that He may work.

Need I at any length remind my reader that this view of the operation of *the Spirit* as the secret of the fruit of holiness leaves wholly inviolate the primary truth that " *Christ* is our Life " ?   We saw early in our Col. iii. 4. enquiry[2] how clear and full is the certainty of that truth ; that while the Spirit of God is the Life-Giver the Son of God is the Life.   But then, the Spirit *is* the Life-GIVER. By Him, in His infinitely gracious personal operation, you and I " have the 1 John v. 12. Son."   And His own divine vital connexion with the Son is such that where He is, savingly, there Christ is, and where Christ is there He is.   If I may quote words of my own written elsewhere : " The Spirit is the eternal and divine personal Vehicle ; Jesus Christ, ' who is our Life,' is the Thing conveyed. . . .   To

---

[1] I use the word Quietism to express *one side of truth*, and only so.   In the history of theological language it has some associa-tions with dangerous error.

[2] Pp. 39, etc.

borrow an imperfect analogy from physical
science, Christ is as the Sun of the soul, the
Spirit is as the luminiferous Ether by whose
vibration we have the Sun's light and heat." [1]

And now we come to St Paul's delineation
of this pure and sweet Fruit of the Spirit. Let
us take it up for a few very practical enquiries
and remarks.

The first point for observation, an obvious
one, but none the less to be definitely considered, is that the Fruit of the Spirit consists
in its essence not of doing but of being. There
is nothing in this description which directly
speaks of energetic enterprise, multiplied labours,
severe sufferings, great material sacrifices. The
activities of life are in fact almost absent from
the immediate view, and the passive, the patient,
aspect of the spiritual man's contact with life
and men is alone very visibly present.

What do we read in this? That the spiritual
man is called, as his highest calling, to cut
himself off from active, willing, practical service
of others? That the celestial fruit will grow,

---

[1] *Outlines of Christian Doctrine*, p. 136. I may refer also to
Thoughts on the Spiritual Life, pp. 60, 61.

and ripen, and be ready for the festival of God, most favourably in a "life of contemplation," in a desert, or a cloister, or a jealously isolated study? The whole New Testament negatives such a thought. In it, the ideal Christian life is the life in which the Lord is glorified and manifested amidst the manifold relative duties and labours of the life of home, of citizenship, of public ministry, of active evangelization. It is a life in which the cross is daily carried,—the cross not of our wilful and ambitious choosing but of the Lord's humbling and searching allotment in the daily path. If the life of a monastery were contemplated in the New Testament at all, as it is not, surely it would be presented there as a "counsel" not "of perfection" but of imperfection; a lower path of surrender and of service, while the higher path was that of the mother, the child, the servant, who in the midst of common life "did the will of God from the soul." Eph. vi. 6.

But then, the impartial Gospel does not say that work is therefore life. It points to the eternal necessity of right being in order to right doing. It bids the Christian live to serve, but live *behind his service* in and with his Lord and Life. It asks, ultimately, not whether

1 Cor. xiii. 3. you give your goods to the poor, or your body to the fire, but whether you love.

So "the Fruit of the Spirit" is a divinely given and developed CHARACTER, drawn out of the fulness of Christ; a character which must express itself in service, but whose

Col. iii. 3. essence "is hid with Christ in God." This is the "fruit" which, according to the Lord Jesus Christ's own words, we shall surely bear if by the Spirit "we abide

John xv. 4-8. in Him." Of this fruit, says the same Teacher, we are to bear "much," to the glory of His Father. We may or may not, in His providence, have much to do for Him in enterprise, in effort, in public testimony, in memorable suffering. Perhaps His will for us, as we submit ourselves wholly to it, humbly ready to "toil and not faint" in His name, may be to do the most silent of domestic duties, or to bear the most exhausting weakness or pain in a neglected sick-room. But these questions touch the accidents of the matter, not the essence. The "fruit" is the

character drawn for us by the Holy Spirit from
Jesus Christ our Head. The "much fruit"
is that character not stunted and dwarfed by
the frosts of unbelief, but expanding in sweet
and strong development in the sunny open air
of the simplest faith.

And now we will look at the particulars of
the description, at the elements which this
inspired analysis shows us in the texture of
this fruit· of Paradise grown on earth.

Those elements are nine : " Love, joy, peace,
longsuffering, gentleness, goodness, faithfulness,
meekness, self-control.[1]" And we may without over-refinement trace a threefold grouping
in the nine. " Love, joy, peace," if I read
their reference aright, describe the character
in its immediate relation to the Lord, who is
its spring of " love," its cause of " joy," its
living law of internal " peace." " Longsuffering, gentleness, goodness," describe it in its
relations with men, as the Christian comes
evermore from the " secret of the Ps. xxxi. 20.
Presence " to live his " hidden " life, unharmed

---

[1] Ἐγκράτεια.

and bearing blessing with it, amidst " the plotting of men " and " the strife of tongues." " Faithfulness, meekness, self-control," denote the Christian's characteristics not so much under the trials of opposition or provocation as in the common calls and duties of the day. And so the " fruit " appears in its fair roundness and ripeness. So the man, born of the Spirit, led of the Spirit, taking step by step by the Spirit, filled with this same blessed Spirit (a " filling " of which we shall say more in the next chapter), lives, moves, and has his being, with and for God and man. He is one personality, and so his regenerate and Spirit-developed character is one, from the " love " to the " self-control " ; from his inmost intercourse with his Lord to his act of most watchful and practical self-discipline in open human life. What he is as indeed a Christian, *in toto*, that is the Spirit's Fruit.

As we close, let us observe some main truths about our Christian character, conveyed to us in this view of the Fruit of the Spirit.

First, it is a character essentially of love and

light. There are other qualifying facts about
it assuredly. There is in the true Christian
a gravity, an earnestness, a recollectedness, the
lack of which would put the man out of
character. This we have set before us here
in the word "temperance," self-control. But
the material, the essence, of the life and
character thus governed and controlled is
"love, joy, peace." Let the disciple remember this, and see that nothing hinders the
manifestation of it. He is a man in whom
dwells that Spirit whose special function it is
to "pour out the *love* of God in the Rom. v. 5.
heart." That Spirit was shed upon the exalted
Head as "the oil of *gladness*," and Heb. i. 9.
as such He flows down upon the member of
that Head to give him "*joy* in the Rom xiv. 17;
Holy Ghost." And He is the Dove see Phil. iii. 3.
of divine *peace*; His "mind" is Rom. viii. 6.
"peace" as well as "life;" He is "the Spirit
of faith," and "peace" as well as 2 Cor. iv. 13.
"joy" comes by "believing." His Rom. xv. 13.
unhindered in-working must come out then in
a life which the known love of God makes
loving—loving towards the Lord, and, in the

Lord, towards men ; *joyful,* with a calm but contagious and beneficent happiness, in its blessed certainty of Christ possessed in His glorious fulness ; and *peaceful,* with a rest-fulness which cannot but diffuse itself around, as the Spirit shows our spirit that "we have

Rom. v. 1.   peace with God," and that the "peace of God" can indeed "keep our hearts

Phil. iv. 7.   and thoughts, in Christ Jesus." Let us remember, let us · yield ourselves up, that we may manifest this essential threefold bright-ness of the life and character of the spiritual man. The Holy Ghost, giving us possession of Christ, is the heavenly Antidote to coldness, to "unpleasantness," to reserve of sympathies and service, to melancholy, to beclouding "worry." Self-control may have to carve deep lines in heart and life ; but the chisel need never deface the brightness of the material.

Again, the character of the spiritual man is, in the relations of man with man, a character which is essentially ready to give way, to for-bear, to bear. No elaborate qualification is needed here of this statement. I remember well what energy for service the Holy Spirit can and does impart to the weakest, and what immovable firmness for truth, for principle, He can and does develope in the most sensitive and timid. But deep below such manifestations, where they are indeed His work, there lies in the order of grace the presence, by His in-dwelling, of a tender and willing *surrender to others*, because first to the Lord, of every mere claim and jealousy of self. In proportion to the fulness of the Spirit's in-working Jesus Christ really occupies the throne usurped before by self. And in proportion to that occupation of the throne by its true King the man will be, more than anything else—whatever else he has to be in the direction of activity and firm-ness—" long-suffering, gentle, good."

Lastly, the truly spiritual character will, in its God-given development, issue always in a practical and wakeful life. Bright with a secret happiness, long-suffering with a deep and genuine surrender, the spiritual man will be "*faithful*" [1] in every particular of duty. He

---

[1] That the word πίστις in this passage means "faithfulness" not "faith" is clear by its collocation with words in which rela-tive duties are plainly in view. See, *e.g.*, Titus ii. 10.

will be loyal to every promise made or trust undertaken. He will be to be depended on in the business of the day. His correspondents will receive punctual answers ; his friends, faithful and careful counsel. His employers will get a service out of him in which their just interests will be as his own. His servants and dependants will find him watchfully equitable, considerate, and courteous. He will take great care to Rom. xiii. 8. "owe no man anything." His church and parish will be truly served, be they ever so large, or small, or unresponsive. He will be known to be one who will take trouble for others, and who is glad to be their servant indeed for Jesus' sake. He will be "*meek*," in the sense of a jealous avoidance of a manner and habit of self-assertion among his brethren in matters of opinion or of work. And with and over it all he will be "*self-controlled.*" He will, for the glory of his Master, and that he may be truly serviceable among his fellows for Him, watch and pray over his own acts and habits ; over bed, and board, and literature, and companionship, and recreation, and imagination, and tongue. Not that he will try to exercise the Stoic's fancied empire of self over self; but he will humbly, recollectedly, with decision, bring the whole of his life, hour by hour, to his glorious Master for orders' and for discipline. He will "keep under his body, and 1 Cor. ix. 27. bring it into subjection," by a steadily maintained surrender of it as "a living Rom. xii. 1. sacrifice," in all its faculties, to Him of whom it is written, "the body is for the 1 Cor. vi. 13. Lord, and the Lord for the body." For the spiritual man, a true self-surrender is the deep secret of a true self-control.

So we shut the Epistle, and close our enquiry into the Fruit of the Spirit. But we will do so only to turn again to life with a fuller recollection of what is the character we are intended to bear as spiritual men, and what is the divine provision, present and perfect, for the being of that character in us and its manifestation by us.

We will take this Scripture to be to us, amongst other things, a touchstone of our spiritual health. Not long ago I heard of a pious and devoted woman who used it habitually for this purpose. If in any degree conscious of a decline or obscuration in her life and work for her Lord, she took Gal. v. 22, 23, and read the words over as in His presence, and asked herself before Him in what particular of the Fruit of the Spirit any recent failure was apparent. Such asking and finding led at once to a repentant renewal of surrender and of faith, and so back to the rest, and to the readiness, which· are for us, by the Holy Ghost, in Jesus Christ our Life.

CHAPTER XI.

WE are still engaged upon the revelation through St Paul of the Holy Spirit and His work. In the present chapter we take up a group of Pauline words and phrases on the subject, rich in materials for enquiry and for faith.

And, first, and mainly, the FULNESS OF THE SPIRIT. The precise phrase is not Pauline; indeed it is not verbally Biblical. But equivalent expressions are abundant, in many parts of Scripture. In the Mosaic age we find the sacred artificer Bezaleel "filled with Exod. xxxi. 3. the Spirit of God" for the work of constructing and adorning the Tabernacle, whose true Designer was none other than Heb. ix. 8. the Holy Spirit. In the Gospel age the Lord Jesus Himself is seen going up from Baptism to Temptation "full of the Luke iv. 1

14

Holy Ghost." His Forerunner was "filled
Luke i. 15,67,41. with the Holy Ghost, even from his
mother's womb." And both the father and
mother of the second Elijah were on special
occasions "filled with the Holy Ghost." At
Pentecost the gathered company, apparently
the "hundred and twenty" of Acts i. 15,
Acts ii. 4. were "all filled with the Holy
Ghost." Peter was specially "filled" when
he met the Jewish Council for the first time,
Acts iv. 8, 31. witnessing to his Lord ; and so,
immediately afterwards, were all the brethren.
Acts ix. 17. So was Paul at his baptism, and
when he sentenced Elymas to blindness. So
Acts xiii. 9, 32. were the disciples at the Pisidian
Antioch in their hour of trial and joy. The
Acts vi. 3. seven "Deacons" were chosen as
" men of honest report, full of the Holy
Ghost and wisdom." And Stephen, in the
Acts vii. 55. act of confession, "being full of the
Holy Ghost, saw heaven opened." Barnabas
Acts xi. 24. is described as a man "full of the
Holy Ghost and of faith."

Such are the main Scriptural parallels which
by way of illustration may be gathered around

the great Pauline passage on the Fulness of
the Spirit, Eph. v. 18 : " Be not drunk with
wine, wherein is excess, but *be ye filled in the
Spirit.*"

Let us approach the text through the avenue
of the parallels, and ask what they have to tell
us on this great and precious fact and phenomenon of the New Life.

In the first place we gather very plainly that
"the Filling" is not identical in idea, whether
or no it coincides in time, with the initial work
of the Spirit as the Life-Giver. The Filling is
always seen as taking place where there is
already present the New Birth; and the possession of that Birth is thus the occasion for a
holy desire and longing to possess in some
sense the Filling.

Again we gather that there are upon the
whole two main aspects or phases of the
Fulness of the Spirit. There is a special, critical, phase, in which at a great crisis it comes
out in marked, and perhaps wholly abnormal, manifestation, as when it enables the man
or woman to utter supernatural prediction

or proclamation.   And there is also what we
may call the habitual phase, where it is used
to describe the condition of this or that believer's life day by day and in its normal course.
Thus the Seven were not so much specially
"filled" as known to be "full;" and so was
Barnabas.   Into this holy habitual fulness Paul
entered, it appears, at his baptism.   On the
other hand the same Paul experienced from
time to time the other and abnormal sort of
filling; and it thus results that the same man
might in one respect be full while in another he
needed to be filled.

There is a close connexion from one point of
view between the Fulness of the Spirit and
what we commonly mean by miraculous powers
and works, particularly the miraculous work
of infallibly "inspired" speaking.   The immediate result at Pentecost was an instantaneous
Acts. ii. 4.   "speaking with other tongues, as
the Spirit gave them utterance."   St Peter,
St Paul, St Stephen, all spoke supernatural
words of testimony, or authority, or vision,
when thus "filled with the Spirit."   The
Lord Jesus Himself in the Fulness of the

Spirit sustained six weeks of fasting and met the Tempter under mysterious conditions. And some may think that we should infer a similar reference wherever the Fulness is spoken of; as if it implied a miracle-working power for instance in the Pisidian Christians, or in the Ephesians who are here enjoined to be "filled in the Spirit."

But it seems clear that this inference is by no means necessary. And the proof of this statement lies in the general testimony of the Word of God, which now in successive chapters we have been collecting, to the character of the *highest ranges* of the Holy One's work. Those highest ranges have to do with not the miraculous, in our common sense of that word, but the moral; the transfiguration of the will, of the heart, of the soul, by the immediate action of the Lord the Spirit. And there would be surely an anomaly, a disproportion, in a real *appropriation* of the glorious phraseology of His FULNESS to the abnormal and (from a true view-point) not noblest and most perfect kind of His operation. As we study the description of the Fruit of the Spirit, and (what will be

before us in our closing chapter) the Indwelling
of Christ in the heart by the Spirit, we are
surely right in being certain that, whatever the
Fulness has to do with tongues and prophecies,
it has its very highest concern with the believer's
spiritual knowledge of His glorious Lord in the
life of faith, and with the true manifestation of
that life in the loveliness of a holy walk.   To be
filled with the Spirit is a phrase intensely connected with the fulness of our consecration to
the will and work of God in human life.

I would not be mistaken, as if I meant to
relegate off-hand to the apostolic age alone
all manifestations of the presence and power
of God through His people in the way of sign
and wonder.   I do gather, both from the
history of the Church and from that pregnant
Scripture, 1 Cor. xiii. 8, that *on the whole* the
commonly called miraculous displays of that
power were intended for the first days only,
or at least in a degree altogether peculiar.
That period had characteristic conditions and
needs which can never quite recur, even where
the Gospel is a new thing among the heathen
of our time.   For the Gospel was then every-

where and absolutely new, with no history
as yet behind it, no results of long years to
give it their credentials. I do not think, with
some earnest Christians, that the Christian
Church is "responsible" for the abeyance of
miraculous manifestation, by a lack of faith
while faith might at any time claim the
wonder-working power. I believe on the
other hand that subtle dangers and strong
temptations lie concealed where the Christian,
or the community, is eager for the gift of such
miraculous faculties rather than for an ever-
deepening abasement of self before the Holy
One and an ever closer and more chastened
walk with Him. But meanwhile it is no part
of such convictions to deny *à priori* the possibility of signs and wonders in any age, our
own or another, since the apostolic. Only
it seems to me to be certain not merely that
upon the whole such operation is not the will
of God now as it was of old, but that this is
so because more and more His people are to
be led in His plan of teaching to rest in that
" more excellent way " which already in that
wonderful first age the Apostle preferred to

₁ Cor. xii. 31. even " the best gifts" of the other kind.[1]

But let us now take up the Apostle's word to the Ephesians : *Be ye filled with the Spirit;* πληροῦσθε ἐν Πνεύματι.

It will be seen, as we look into the context, and as we recall what has now been said on the two phases of manifestation of the Fulness, that we have here a precept not for a crisis but for the whole habit of the Christian's life. Not the least reference to works of wonder occurs in the context. " Psalms, and hymns, and spiritual songs," are the manifestation of the Fulness specially and at once in view, and the blessed habit of thankfulness, and the habitual readiness to forget self in the interests of others, and then all the lovely details of the life of a sanctified home. And we must observe that the preceptive verb (πληροῦσθε) is in the present or continuing tense. It enjoins a course, a habit, not a critical effort or venture. It lays it upon

---

[1] I commend to the reader's attention the late Dean Goode's *Modern Claims to the Possession of the Extraordinary Gifts of the Spirit, stated and examined* (1834).

the believer so to use the open spiritual secrets
of his life in the Lord as to enter upon and
walk in a state of divine Fulness which shall
be, above all things, useful and rich in blessing
for the needs of the daily path, and shall
result, whatever else it results in, in a temper
of continual modesty and unselfish serviceable-
ness towards all around him. We must observe
further the exact wording of the phrase in
its last words : " Be ye filled *in* the Spirit, ἐν
Πνεύματι."   It is as if the Apostle had written
at large, " Be filled *with* that Holy Spirit *in*
whom you are ; you *are in* the Spirit, if so
be that the Spirit of God dwell in   Rom. viii. 9.
you ; see now to it that by His grace you
are in such relations of faith and submission
with Him that He who is within you shall
be no longer, if hitherto, a well-head hidden
beneath the *débris* of disobedience and unbelief, but springing, rising, unhindered in
His blessed overflow, till *all* regions of the
inner man ' live ' indeed where that ' river
cometh ; ' till *all* parts of your   Ezek. xlvii. 9.
outward walk and work are ruled by the
Spirit of God, and a holy abundance goes

John vii. 38, 39. forth through you to the blessing of the souls of others."

Such, I believe is a simple account of the Fulness of the Spirit as it is presented here in this divine word of appeal, exhortation, and implied promise. The Apostle in effect calls Rom. vi. 13. upon the believer to "yield himself unto God" the Holy Ghost as to a Power and Presence already dwelling in living reality within him, but waiting, as it were, for the welcome of the soul to come forth from within and take entire possession of the whole circle and range of life. It is no invitation to a spasmodic or tempestuous enthusiasm. It is a call to let the water from the mountain-springs of God rise in the man, in his purposes, in his affections, in his works, in his will, calmly and surely towards its blessed level.

Let us not forget the holy reality under its sacred imagery. This appeal of the Spirit by St Paul is sent straight to the innermost heart of my reader, and of myself. What does it mean in our life, as that life is to be lived this day? By grace we believe in the Son of God revealed. Therefore most surely the Spirit is in us, for without His inworking we should never have "called Jesus Lord." But are 1 Cor. xii. 3. we filled, nay are we filling, with the Spirit? IsH is blessed power upon our "first springs of thought and will" a power fully welcomed there? Are we watching and praying over the matter, and humbly resolved, looking up for light, that nothing we know of in act, or habit, in occupation, in recreation, in thought and word about our neighbour, in use of time or means, is such as to obstruct the rise of His "calm excess" through all we are and all we have? St Paul calls us to this humble and holy watching and resolve; and assuredly the whole Word of God promises a blissful result, to the glory not of ourselves but of our Lord, upon our so doing in His name.

So let us do then, in the name of Jesus Christ. As I said, this precept implies a promise. And the promise is unto not great or exceptional Christians, but to the Christian—who yields himself to God. At Ephesus, it was meant for the everyday Christian believer; husband, wife, parent, child, master, slave. They were all meant to live lives divinely full, full from within ;

> "Not roughened by those cataracts and breaks
> Which humour interposed so often makes ; "

and which are made indeed by anything and everything in which the soul at all rebels against the Holy Ghost ; but equal, equable, under the welcomed power of the Lord. And what this precept meant at Ephesus it means in England, it means to the man who writes these words in his study at Cambridge, and to his brother in Christ who reads them wherever God has bid him dwell.

Are our lives " full " with the fulness of multiplied duties, of heavy calls upon every hour ? Let us calm them and illuminate them with this other Fulness in its divine simplicity. Let the Spirit, the Life-Giver, the Revealer of Christ, the Imparter of Christ to us, have His way, and rise and fill the man. Then the life full of toil will be a life full also of internal peace.

It will be in place here to remark on the phrase the BAPTISM OF THE SPIRIT. That phrase is not precisely Pauline. We have only an approach to it in the words, " by one Spirit we were all baptized into 1 Cor. xii. 13. one body." But its connexion with the subject of the Fulness of the Spirit, as seen in the Ephesian Epistle, is close and important. It occurs in each of the Gospels Matt. iii. 11. Mark i. 8. and twice in the Acts. It will be Luke iii. 16. John i. 26, 33. seen that the Lord Jesus appears Acts i. 5, xi. 16. there always as the Baptizer. And it will be seen also that while the mentions of the holy Filling are frequent the recorded occasions of the Baptism are two only; the Day of Pentecost, and the closely parallel occasion when in the house of Cornelius St See Acts xi. 15, Peter, the Apostle of Pentecost, was 16. permitted solemnly and for ever to " open the door of faith to the Gentiles." Nowhere in the Epistles does the precise phrase " Baptism of the Spirit" occur. Are we not thus led to the conclusion that the Baptism is not to be identified with the Filling, and is not, like the Filling, presented to us as a blessing for which the Christian is to seek ?

I am aware that the question is not without

its special difficulties. The analogy of the
Sacrament of Baptism would in itself lead us to
connect the Baptism of the Spirit rather with
the beginning of the new life than with a great
development of it ; but we can hardly do this
without reserve, in view of the fact that the
Apostles themselves were not till the Day of
Pentecost subjects of this Baptism. Still, both
the Pentecost and the Visit to Cornelius were
not only historical events but great representative occasions, each of which was as it were a
birth-time of the true Church by the power of
the Spirit. And each may thus be held to
typify and signify on a great scale the true
birth-process and birth-time, by the same
power, in the case of the individual soul. Anywise it is remarkable and significant that the
developed teaching of the Epistles contains
no appeal to the man already in Christ to seek
the Baptism of the Spirit. We are to be filled,
and to be full of Him, as those who have
already received Him " from the height that
knows no measure."

In view of these facts of Scripture may I say,
with tenderness and deep spiritual sympathy,

that a mistake appears to underlie the practice, not uncommon now among earnest Christians, of *waiting* for a special " Baptism of the Spirit " in order to more effectual service for the Lord ? Surely, "by one Spirit we *have been baptized* into one body."   And now our part 1 Cor. xii. 13. is to open in humblest faith all the avenues and regions of the soul and of the life, that we may be filled with what we already have.[1]

And how shall this be done ?   St Paul gives the answer : " That we might re- Gal. iii. 14. ceive the promise of the Spirit *through faith.*"   Yes, through faith, the mouth of the inner man, "opened" that He Ps. lxxxi. 10. who has promised may " fill " it.   In this brief, loving appeal to the Ephesian saints, the Apostle does but ask them to open and

---

[1] I may refer to an admirable little tract in verse by an anonymous Writer ; *The Baptism of the Holy Ghost.*   The tract is "to be had of the Secretary of the *Mildmay Letter Mission,* 66, Mildmay Park, London."   A short quotation shows what its drift is :—

> "Thine is the throne-room of the soul !
>   Its Ruler, break each barrier down ;
> As with full tide o'erflood the whole,
>   Self overborne by Thee alone : . . .
> Spirit of truth, of holiness,
> We cry not '*enter*,' but '*possess*.'"

receive ; to take their stand upon a promise. Not by mighty spiritual effort but in order to it is that "promise" to be "received." We are to take the Lord at His word, to trust Him to bless us fully in His keeping His word. We are to open to Him all the inner doors of the soul, the chamber doors, as we have opened the main portal. And we are to use the same key, "the key of promise," which is, from the other point of view, the key of our simplest and most confiding faith.

Believing, we receive. And blessed then will be the manifestations of the holy Gift received, in one special direction and another. We shall know something of what it is to be Rom. xv. 13. "filled with all joy and peace in believing, that we may abound in hope, by the power of the Holy Ghost." We shall be Phil. i. 11. on our way to be "filled with the fruit of righteousness ; " "filled with the Col. i. 9. knowledge of His will." We shall be realizing something indeed, by the power of Him who is the Bond betwixt us and our Head, of that Filling which we already possess (but possession is not realization) in Him in

whom "all the Fulness dwells." Yes, we shall
be filled, we shall be filling, in our _{Col. i. 29 with}
finite receptivity, with that " Fulness ^{ii. 10.}
of God" which means whatsoever Eph. iii. 19.
being glory in Him is capable of becoming
grace in us.

Here will be a blessed and continuous answer
to the prayer of our Communion Service, that
wonderful and pregnant petition : "We humbly
beseech Thee that all we, who are partakers of
this holy Communion, may be FUL-FILLED with
Thy grace and heavenly benediction."

Let us not forget the words which, with
profound significance, just precede that prayer :
"Here we offer and present unto Thee, O
Lord, ourselves, our souls and bodies, to be a
reasonable, holy, and lively sacrifice unto Thee."
We yield ourselves to Him for His will. He
meets us with His sacred Fulness.

To this same range of truth we may refer the language of St Paul about
the SEALING by the Spirit, and the
EARNEST of the Spirit, and the
FIRSTFRUITS of the Spirit. No doubt the

Eph. i. 13, 14 ;
iv. 30.
2 Cor. i. 22.
Rom. viii. 23.

15

" Gifts " of the primeval Church are considerably in view in each of those phrases. But surely the same reasons which have constrained us to apply[1] the Apostle's language about the Fulness to the " more excellent way " of the divine life of faith, hope, and love, apply here. The believer, already a believer by the Spirit's lifegiving operation, is now also " sealed " as the property of his Master by the same Spirit's developed possession of Him. And this possession, with its holy fruit, is the " earnest " of his full possession of his God for ever in eternity ; the " first-fruits " Gal. vi. 8. of the harvest of " life everlasting " which is to be reaped " of the Spirit " then at length.

Come forth then, eternal Spirit, and be ever coming forth, from Thy secret place within our spirit, into all that we are, and all that we have, to fill all in all in us, and to overflow through us. Fill Thou us in a blessed continuousness and habit, enabling us in humble continuousness to

---

[1] Page 215.

receive Thee, day by day and hour by hour, through faith. At each crisis of need fill us with Thy special fulness out of Thy habitual. And when the hour of death shall come, so fill us that we may see with our spirit's eyes, in Thy light, heaven opened, and the Son of Man standing at the right hand of God. Amen.

CHAPTER XII.

FOR the main theme of our enquiry in the last chapter we went to the Epistle to the Ephesians. And now, for the last of our successive explorations of this continent of living truth, we come to the same Epistle again, and to a passage more full if possible than even that other of the inmost treasures of the doctrine of the Spirit.

Who has not read and re-read the closing verses of the third chapter of the Ephesians with the feeling of one permitted to look through parted curtains into the Holiest Place of the Christian life ? Who has not longed to step into that sanctuary in a personal experience of its riches and blessings ? Who that in any true sense has entered in by grace does not feel, does not know, that indeed it is rest and joy beyond all exposition to be there ?

It is the spiritual *summum bonum* of the
Pilgrimage. It is the beginning of the happiness of the eternal Country.

Approaching this very sacred passage for
some special meditations on one glorious part
of it, let us first briefly recall its contents as a
whole.

It forms the resumption of a dropped subject.
At the close of ch. ii. the Apostle had written
of the building of the great spiritual Temple,
the true Church of God, the holy structure in
which every stone is living and in living contact
with the *Angulare Fundamentum*, the Stone of
the Corner. That structure he had described
as rising, growing, "into an holy sanctuary in
the Lord ; " preparing for the eternal Day of
its final consecration, when it should be ready
at length and for ever to be the " abiding
habitation of God in the Spirit." Eph. ii. 22.
Then followed a long and memorable digression, in which the imagery of sanctuary and
habitation disappears. But at the fourteenth
verse of the next chapter, our present chapter,
it comes up again. We read again, and in a
like connexion with the work and grace of

Father, Son, and Holy Ghost, of a "perma-
nent inhabitation."[1] We see again a divine
Indweller, abiding in a shrine constructed as
it were of human materials and prepared for
His presence by the skill and power of the
Spirit. But there is a difference. The former
passage had to do rather with the believing
Company as such, the Temple of the true
Church. This has to do rather with that com-
pany as seen in its individuals; it speaks of the

Eph. iii. 17. *"hearts"* of the saints, a word full
of the thought of separate personalities; it contemplates them as each an abode for the divine
Indwelling. Each living stone is as it were
taken by itself, and seen as a miniature of the
Living Temple; not so that the glorious total
is forgotten, for it appears throughout the whole
passage in the use of the plural ("your *hearts,*"

Eph. iii. 18. and "with *all saints*"), but so that
the individual aspect of the matter is the most
prominent for the time. This form of the divine
Inhabiting St Paul here dwells upon, and suppli-

Eph. iii. 16. cates the Father of the great Family

---

[1] The κατοικῆσαι of iii. 17 takes up the κατοικητήριον of ii. 22.

that by the Spirit it may take place fully and
decisively in each Ephesian disciple. And then
he proceeds to prayer on prayer, all <small>Eph. iii. 17-21.</small>
springing from this same root of blessing. He
asks that the saints, thus each possessed by
Christ as perpetual Inhabitant, "rooted and
grounded" in that eternal Love which is
manifested and conveyed through Him, may
all together in some sort grasp the measureless
dimensions of that Love, and all get a new and
blissful knowledge in particular of the Love
of Christ Himself, and all be filled with "the
Fulness of God," with "the plenitude of those
blessings which the Infinite One is willing and
able to bestow at each moment upon the finite
recipient." Then follows that great Doxology
in which "glory is given," now and in the
endless prospect, to the Father of the Son and
of the saints in Him, in view of His almighty
and unmeasured power to bless, and of the
coming eternal manifestation of His praise " in
the Church, and in Christ Jesus." [1]

We have thus in some slight sense traversed

---

[1] I use the preferable reading here, ἐν τῇ ἐκκλησίᾳ καὶ ἐν Χριστῷ
Ἰησοῦ.

the paragraph and reviewed its outline. I do so partly because there is a sort of sacred necessity to do so; to be so near such treasures of revealed grace and life, and to say nothing about the rest of them because our precise concern is with only one or two, is at least difficult. But also this view of the passage as a whole brings out what I would wish to remember throughout our present enquiry, that the profoundly individual blessing and experience with which we are specially concerned is set forth in connexion with more than individual interests. It is a thing which does not terminate in the saint ; it goes out through him to "all the saints," and it finds its rest and goal in the glory of God.

But now to come to the treasures of truth which are our immediate subject. They are, the Dwelling of Christ in the heart by faith, and the connexion of this great gift of grace with a special work of the HOLY SPIRIT.

Let me speak very simply, and at no great length, of the Inhabitation of the Lord in the heart. The theme is one rather for believing and adoring prayer, and reception, and experience, than for much explanation or disquisition. A few great points stand out however so clearly from the words that I may reverently say a little of them, as in the presence of our Lord the Indweller.

First we plainly have here a truth more special than the underlying truth that "in" every true believer Christ is, by the Holy Spirit. Precious beyond all estimate is that truth, and happy the man who habitually remembers it and acts upon it. Yes; "Jesus Christ is in you, except ye be 2 Cor. xiii. 5. counterfeits;" and great indeed are the inferences meant to flow direct from that fact into the Christian's faith and life.[1] But there is something more special here. For these Ephesians are addressed as no counterfeits in spiritual life; and yet St Paul prays that Christ may dwell in their hearts.

Secondly, the kind of speciality is indicated by the word "your *hearts;*" not your nature, your being, but your hearts. And " the heart"

---

[1] See above, ch. ii.

is a word which, in Scripture, means very much
the organ of the whole inner consciousness, of
living thought, affection, will.   Accordingly the
Indwelling here must be something appropriate
to that organ ; a blessed Presence of the Lord
in the saint's recollection, and love, and purposes.   "In" the Christian off his guard the
Lord still "is," in His patient mercy ; but not
"dwelling in his heart."   To borrow the
imagery of a Puritan commentator[1] on the
Ephesian Epistle, Christ may be present in
the Temple, in the Church, of the believer's
being, while yet He is not sitting enthroned
in its Choir.

Thirdly, the words of the Apostle assure
us that it is the plan and purpose of the Gospel
that such a session of Christ in the sanctuary
of affections and will should be the experience,
and the abiding experience, of every disciple.
Not some of the Ephesian saints but all of
them are contemplated in this great prayer ; in
each heart of all the company Christ is thus
to abide.   No esoteric privilege, to be won by

---

[1] Bayne, or Baynes, of Cambridge ; *obiit* 1617.

special achievements, or by special austerities, or under exceptional surroundings, is here in view. The means of attainment, or rather of reception, are divinely simple, as we shall presently see ; this sacred bliss of the Presence is to be entered upon "by faith." And it is meant to be not an intermittent and precarious glory, dropped for a season through the rolling clouds of doubt and fear, and soon to fade again into twilight. The word [1] selected to describe it is a word made expressly to denote residence as against lodging, the abode of a master within his own home as against the turning "aside for a night" of the Jer. xiv. 8. wayfarer who will be gone to-morrow. Holy and welcome intimation ! It is within the scope of prayer, and of humblest expectation, and of believing reception, that this most sacred Presence of our Lord, in a mode which affects the inmost experience of His servant, shall be as continuous and as regular (may I not venture to say ?) as the very consciousness of our own personality. "Even so, come, Lord Jesus."

---

[1] Κατοικεῖν.

Lastly, the grammatical shape here of this same verb, its aorist tense,[1] suggests to the reader the thought not only of a divine Indwelling in the heart, but of a certain *coming in* of the Indweller, a *taking up* of His holy residence within. It conveys the idea of an initial entrance in order to a stated permanence of presence. And the inquiry presents itself, whether this teaches us that for each Christian, in the law of his spiritual life, there is intended to take place at some stage of his progress a definite and solemn step from a lower to a higher experience, from an ordinary to an extraordinary state of communion with his Lord. Did St Paul view the Ephesians as all then occupying a lower level from which they were all to rise decisively and forthwith to another as yet unknown to them ? I cannot think that his meaning can be put precisely thus, in view of the whole context, and of his whole teaching. I do not trace in the New Testament at large any formed and deliberate doctrine of such a single and ruling crisis as

---

[1] Κατοικῆσαι.

divinely intended in every case of life and
faith, and accordingly to be sought by every
convert. The blessing indicated has nothing
in it to forbid that it should coincide with
the earliest living acceptance of Christ by the
awakened man ; and it has nothing in it to
forbid the belief that in countless instances
it should be truly present while yet its arrival,
its development, was unnoticed by the man
and took place through a process which he
cannot even seem to analyse. Let no Christian
judge another in this matter. But then let no
Christian whose record is thus *uniformitarian*
(if we may borrow a word from the geologist)
think that for his friend or brother there cannot be a critical and decisive experience of the
Indweller's " arrival to reside in the heart."
Testimonies innumerable, and given by gravest
witnesses, tell us that such experienced arrivals
of Jesus Christ there are, followed by a residence in the heart which is indeed a new and
blissful experience to the man, as he discovers
that what has before been an occasional and
exceptional communion of soul with His living
and present Redeemer may be, and in fact

proves to be, prevailing and habitual. Such
cases St Paul I doubt not contemplates here,
assured that within the large community at
Ephesus there were many for whom such a
crisis was the great spiritual need. And he
includes the whole company in his prayer;
partly, if I read him aright, to remind each
disciple that whatever might be his experience
of the Arrival there was no man who might
not possess, and ought not to possess, the
experience of the Presence; but partly for
another reason. The holy Reality, in this as
in other things of the soul, inevitably tran-
scended any single metaphor of it. Arrival
and Residence were ideas not narrowly to be
limited to any one crisis of the life of faith,
however great and memorable. Even for the
most fully experienced, each access of conscious
knowledge of the power of that Presence in
the heart would be as it were a new arrival
for another stay. Such is HE of whom the
writer speaks, and such is His indwelling, that
in the very heart itself, in the very same heart,
He may from one point of view be lastingly
present while from another point of view He

may be arriving even now. " Even so come, Lord Jesus."

But while we thus speak of this sacred In-dwelling, this dear inner secret of the Christian life, are we forgetting our true theme, the work of the Holy Spirit? No, we are not. I have dwelt thus far upon ver. 17 in order to put with the more emphasis the truth of ver. 16, the revealed action of the Spirit in this matter.

Observe then that it is HE who so to speak stands behind this whole wonderful experience as its immediate Agent and Secret. The Apostle bows his knees to the Father that these dear Ephesians, each and all, one by one, may be dealt with in divine speciality by the Holy Ghost. HE must act in them and through them if Christ is thus to dwell within. Deep below the Christian's consciousness, within those springs of thought and will which are such mysteries to the person himself, the Spirit of the Father—and of the Son—must do the work of " strengthening with might in the inner man." Operating there with the divine skill which violates nothing in the nature He has made, and with the divine power which can do what He will in and with that nature, He must give, He will give, supernaturally to the man's inmost self a spiritual firmness and vigour which shall discard certain deep fears and do certain acts that could not otherwise be done.

Sacredly significant indeed is the phraseology. In order to a reception into me of what is altogether the gift of God and not the sequel or remuneration of any toils or endurances of mine, I yet need to be "strengthened with might by the Spirit in" ("*deep* within," as the Greek[1] seems precisely to indicate) "the inner man." And I ask what this means, what is the occasion in this matter for a divine *strengthening*, where perhaps I might have looked rather for such words as subduing or alluring. And I read the answer in the light of the truth that the blessing in question is the residence always in the heart of its MASTER and LORD, who where He dwells must rule ; who enters not to cheer and soothe alone but before all things else to reign. And I remember that nature, nature in the Fall, does not like that Presence in that aspect ; fears greatly to admit "this

---

[1] Εἰς τὸν ἔσω ἄνθρωπον.

Man to reign over us." I remem- Luke xix. 14.
ber that the regenerate soul itself—such is
the dimness of sight and the spiritual im-
becility of even the child of God "in this
tabernacle"—all too easily loses its conscious
certainties of the absolute tenderness along
with the absolute sovereignty and royalty of
the Lord who "stands at the" inner Rev. iii. 20.
"door and knocks;" it trembles lest His in-
coming should of necessity bring some nameless
shock or sorrow in its train. "I dreaded to
yield myself without reserve to Jesus Christ,'
said a Christian kinswoman of my own, relating
to a little circle the story of her own experience; "I felt so sure that He would take from
me my little Hugh." But the strength of a
quiet confidence in the perfect wisdom and love
of the claimant King, along with a calm intuition into His adorable beauty and desirableness,
at length overcame that dread; and the door
was opened, cost what it might. He has come
in—and the child has not been taken from the
mother's embrace, or rather it has been given
back to her, "Isaac-like," more than ever her
own, out of that supreme surrender.

16

Do we not understand in the light of such an instance the need of the Holy Spirit's *strength-giving* work, in order to the reception of the Lord Christ as the abiding and ruling Inhabitant of the very heart? And do we not see how it is the special function of none other than THE SPIRIT so to deal with the inner man? He is the Glorifier of Christ; it is His, as we have seen above,[1] to

> " Show us that loving Man
> That rules the courts of bliss,
> The Lord of hosts, the mighty God,
> The eternal Prince of Peace."

And in the sacred matter of the Indwelling, it is He accordingly who so "shows" Him to the wistful soul that it sees, with an intuition truly its own yet supernatural in its conditions, how safe, how satisfying, how blissful is His all-ruling presence, not only in "the courts of bliss" but in the believing sinner's heart. So the door is opened, for this private but royal entrance of the King of Glory. So work Thou then in us all, O Spirit of the Father and of the Son.

---

[1] Page 120.

And here, as our meditation on this bright oracle closes, let us lastly remember those words of ver. 17 ; "*by faith.*" They are all-important to a practical use of the truth and promise of our Lord's Indwelling. On the one hand they remind us that, if that Indwelling is to be our experience indeed, there is need of genuine personal action on the Christian's own part, action God-taught and God-granted, as we have seen, yet not the less the man's own. The Lord "stands at the door and Rev. iii. 20. knocks ; " the man, the inner man, must rise and set it open. Faith is the act of man though it is "the gift of God ; "[1] and " by Eph. ii. 8. means of faith" Christ arrives in the heart to dwell there. But on the other hand, because the action of the soul *is* in this case faith, and nothing else, the words remind us for our "comfort and good hope" that the action is in effect nothing but the utmost simplicity of reception. Do we need to define " faith " to ourselves over again ?[2] Has not every instance of the use of the word by our

---

[1] See above, p. 106.   [2] See above, p. 108.

Lord Himself in the Gospels long ago assured us that it means just personal reliance, personal trust, personal entrustment [1] ? It is the open arms which in their emptiness embrace Christ, the open lips which receive Him as the bread of the soul, the life, the all. As in Justification so in this its glorious sequel, our part is to take the Promise as it stands, to take the Thing in the envelope of the Promise, and to act upon its holy presence and reality.

Well has it been said that weak faith may indeed do but weak works but that it can— open a door.

And He who is "the Spirit of faith" is 2 Cor. iv. 13. faith's appropriate Giver, for this as for all things. For this, as for our earliest acts of trust, HE enables us, by manifesting Christ in His divine trustworthiness and putting the soul into contact with Him, the seen, the trusted, the welcomed Lord.

> "O Son of God, who lovest me,
> I will be Thine alone ;
> And all I have, and all I am,
> Shall henceforth be Thine own."

---

[1] See Bp O'Brien, *Nature, etc., of Faith*, ch. i.

It is a "full and glad surrender." "And all this hath worked that one and the selfsame SPIRIT."

Our enquiries and meditations on the Person and the Work of the Holy Spirit here draw to a close. It is needless to spend words in owning how fragmentary, how imperfect, even on a very modest standard, the attempt has been. But I can hope and can pray that my reader may have gained here and there a suggestion, perhaps about some forgotten side of a familiar truth, and that he may have felt some stimulus to an ever-deepening search into the divine Word for more and yet more of the treasures of the truth of the Holy Spirit.

And may writer and reader both be found, through His great grace, among the happy ones who, living by the Spirit, walk by the Spirit, and by the Spirit draw continually out of the fulness of Jesus Christ, to whom by the Spirit they are conjoined in an unspeakable union.

More than thirty years ago that great man, great thinker and preacher, and great saint,

Adolphe Monod, lay on his sorely suffering and comparatively early deathbed at Paris. Led in his youth through experiences of complicated doubt and profound melancholy to the foot of the atoning Cross of a divine and personal Redeemer, and to the solemn and glad experiences of the work of the Spirit in the believer's life, and to a holy submission and repose before the whole revealed truth of our salvation by grace, he had spent his years and used all his great gifts of intellect and of heart " in the defence and confirmation of the Gospel," with the one longing, loving desire to bring others into the peace and certainty he had found, and to build them up in it.[1] Now he was dying, at the age of fifty-four. His beloved ministry was over, and he was looking back on work and onward into the heavenly rest from his Pisgah-top of suffering. One day,[2] in the midst of much physical distress, a few words escaped him, his brief

---

[1] An impressive word-portrait of M. Monod is given in M. Guizot's *Méditations sur l'État actuel de la Réligion Chrétienne* (1866), pp. 170-184.

[2] *Vie*, p. 470; *Life and Letters* (English translation), p. 244.

summary of a Christian's peace, strength, aim, and all. I close by repeating them, and invite my reader with me to make them the motto not only of our death hereafter but of our life this day:

"𝔄ll in 𝔗hrist ; by the 𝔥oly 𝔖pirit ; for the 𝔊lory of 𝔊od. 𝔄ll else is nothing."

" Du Athem aus der ew'gen Stille,
    Durchwehe sanft der Seelen Grund ;
Füll' mich mit aller Gottesfülle,
    Und da wo Sünd' und Gräuel stund,
Lass Glaube, Lieb', und Ehrfurcht grünen,
Im Geist and Wahrheit Gott zu dienen.

" O Geist, O Strom, der uns vom Sohne
    Eröffnet, und krystallenrein
Aus Gottes und des Lammes Throne
    Nun quillt in stille Herzen ein,
Ich öffne meinen Mund und sinke
Hin zu der Quelle, das ich trinke."

TERSTEEGEN, 1697—1769.

INDEX OF SUBJECTS AND NAMES.

INDEX OF SCRIPTURES MORE OR LESS EXPLAINED.

PRINTED BY
HAZELL, WATSON, AND VINEY, LD.,
LONDON AND AYLESBURY.